D0434988

COMMITMENTS

Intimate Stories of Love That Lasts

Also by Sheila Gormely:

Drugs and the Canadian Scene

SHEILA GORMELY

COMMITMENTS
Intimate Stories of Love
That Lasts

Doubleday Canada Limited, Toronto, Canada
Doubleday & Company, Inc., Garden City, New York
1982

For my mother, Charlotte Gormely, my husband, Don Obe, and my daughter, Kira.

Library of Congress Cataloging in Publication Data

Gormely, Sheila.
  Commitments: intimate stories of love that lasts.

  1. Marriage—North America. 2. Unmarried couples—North America. 3. Interpersonal relations. 4. Love. 5. Commitment (Psychology) I. Title.
HQ734.G67   306.8
Library of Congress Catalog Card Number 78-22631
ISBN 0-385-14477-6   AACR2

Sections of "Marital Therapy from a Psychiatric Perspective: An Overview," by Ellen M. Berman, M.D., and Harold I. Lief, M.D., are reprinted with permission from the *American Journal of Psychiatry* 132:6 (June 1975).

Contents

INTRODUCTION: The Search for Commitment *vii*

1. PATTERNS OF DEVOTION: The Experts *1*
2. HONORING THE VOWS: Monogamy *28*
3. FORGIVING PEOPLE: Compromise *50*
4. INEVITABLE DALLIANCE: Affairs *68*
5. ONCE MORE WITH FEELING: Second Marriages *87*
6. LOVE THY NEIGHBOR: Open Marriages *110*
7. BOYS AND GIRLS TOGETHER: Homosexuals *127*
8. THE GAUGUIN SYNDROME: Second Careers *147*
9. INTIMATE PARTNERS: Working Together *166*
10. AND GOD MAKES THREE: Religion in Marriage *184*

CONCLUSION: For a Long, Long Time *199*

Introduction
The Search for Commitment

My purpose in writing this book is best expressed in these words by John Cheever:

> I wanted to study triumphs, the rediscoveries of love, all that I know in the world to be decent, radiant, and clear.

As I took to the roads of North America looking for couples who had managed to stay together in an era when love and commitment seem to be endangered species, I kept Cheever's words in front of me. For six months I searched for the "decent, radiant, and clear" couples who exemplified his sentiments, a task that some people felt would defeat me. They were wrong, and in fact these couples were remarkably easy to locate in our cities, suburbs, and countrysides all across the continent. Today, when people ask me, "How did you find them?" I simply reply: "I think they were waiting."

Unlike others today, I don't believe that Cheever or the solid couples I have met are living in the eighties as rare idealists. In fact, they have seen as much as anyone the decay of permanence and endurance. They know that people lose either their jobs or their interest in them; they know that spouses are easily lost; they see their children's fading respect for parenthood; they lose contact with their own parents and their brothers and sisters; they become insular and reach the unenviable conclusion that the only person you can trust is your-self. But no matter how many years of personal voyage it takes, people discover in the end that their destiny is a cave-old thing—to succeed at love and usefulness. This is the prem-ise of my book and I am happy to say that the premise holds.

The idea of talking intimately to people about successful relationships grew out of a magazine article I wrote called "Home to Monogamy." As a woman with a great deal invested in my marriage, I got tired of reading about divorces and ex-tramarital affairs and of seeing some of my friends unable to maintain their relationships. I was trying not to be judgmental and closed-minded about changing social values, but surely, I thought, there have to be couples who live together in sane and pleasurable arrangements. I wanted to determine if the notion of commitment still existed and was workable.

Responses to my article suggested that people are starved for news about good marriages and good relationships and I decided to write a book for them, based on further interviews. I wanted to include not only couples who have traditional, monogamous marriages but also couples who were unmarried or gay, or whose relationships did not depend on sexual fidelity. As long as the couples had a stable relationship and wanted it to last, I wanted to talk to them. The emphasis was on what people perceive commitment to be. I discovered that values such as respect, love, dignity, and selflessness were just as important today as they ever have been.

I decided at the outset not to play the numbers game but to try for quality of interviews. That is why there are no statis-tics to be drawn from the book. I present no more than what the people said when I talked to them; I have also decided not to rely heavily on the opinions of experts in assessing my sub-jects' personalities and life-styles, though I do include a chapter on the current thinking of some experts that I think should be of general interest. While I have found psychiatrists, marriage counselors, and others in the human relations field to be open, articulate, and genuinely concerned about how people cope in changing times, it has always been my belief that ordinary people who are managing to lead decent and reasonably successful lives are often the best experts.

Usually I talked to people as couples, but there were a few individuals who asked to be interviewed without their partners because of some knowledge—infidelity, for example—which they wished to spare them. The ages of my subjects ranged from the twenties through the sixties. I don't like labels—most people don't—but they were middle and upper middle class. Although some had to be more careful about their money than others, none approached the poverty line.

I discovered these people through an ever-expanding grapevine of friends. I assured each couple of complete anonymity (although some wanted me to use their real names) and have used only invented first names to identify them. In some cases where place of residence, profession, or even number of children might make them recognizable I altered some facts, though not sufficiently to distort their essential character.

I cautioned everyone at the outset that interviews would be on a very personal level and that if they were unable to discuss their relationship openly we shouldn't get together. When I asked the people who accepted my invitation why they were willing to be interviewed, a few suggested it was flattering to their egos, but most of the couples just wanted to affirm various vows; they wanted to make it clear that they were proud to be together.

I used no questionnaire but there were obvious subjects that needed to be discussed: the effects of the sexual revolution and women's liberation; the importance of sexual fidelity; the conflict between personal freedom and compromise; individual and mutual expectations; pain and pleasure; and, of course, children. Although I encouraged couples to bring up all major issues in a relationship, I found that in the end the conversation always turned back to sex. Once or twice this prolonged exposure to the subject caused my eyes to glaze over.

I hope the stories told to me by so many different couples will shed some light on how and why some people stay together. It is not the intention of this book to promote any particular life-style; some of the couples' opinions and beliefs may be disturbingly "modern" and a few may seem hopelessly old-fashioned. A psychiatrist summed up what a lot of people are experiencing today and it explains why I feel my subject is so important. He said: "I have never seen such a concentrated search for meaningful relationships and I have never seen such a confused one." I believe that if anything can bring us out of this confusion, it may be the lesson of example.

Finally, I would like to express my gratitude to the people I interviewed. They were unbelievably generous with their thoughts and with their hospitality. It has been some time since I met them and, although I'm not likely to see them again, they are friends in my memory. Many of them told me they enjoyed the interviews and I would like to return the compliment by saying that I was enriched by all of them.

COMMITMENTS

Intimate Stories of Love That Lasts

1

Patterns of Devotion
The Experts

The study of human relations is sharply divided and most theories about behavior can be applauded or dismissed with equal passion and intellect. Yet an increasing number of people consult professional counselors about the new and confusing issues of adult life.

Some people go to experts because they have temporarily lost their ability to make lasting decisions when there is so much freedom available and so many options open in life-style and contemporary standards. Others go because they have developed high expectations for happiness and fulfillment, and when they aren't obtainable they don't know how to deal with their disappointment. But by far, sexual incompatibility is the major problem people bring to a psychiatrist's office and they are usually unaware that this is seldom the only or real cause of the breakdown in relationships. In fact, about 80 per cent of sexual problems are the consequence of all sorts of other dissatisfactions.

The psychiatrists, marriage counselors, and philosophers I talked to for this book were willing to forgo, to a large extent, their particular clinical interests and to talk about the general condition of people. Overall, they see that it is hard work to become a realized person and the struggle isn't helped much by the fact there has been a startling upheaval in the old values and the social rules which used to hold us together. It's difficult enough for individuals to keep in balance; no wonder more and more couples find it rough going not only to stay together, but also to maintain some measure of harmony and joy.

Amid the many opinions expressed by the experts, one seems to be that people, in their infinite variety, still share common needs and beliefs with others. Shifting cultural values don't mean we have to turn our lives upside down. Changes can be assimilated at our own pace and it is not necessary to accept them all. The essential message has always been to understand ourselves, make the adjustments we consider necessary, and then try to be at peace with the people we love.

I asked Dr. Harold I. Lief, professor of psychiatry and director of the Division of Family Studies at the University of Pennsylvania School of Medicine and also director of the Marriage Council of Philadelphia, if he thought sex as an issue in today's relationships was overrated. Sex is significant in itself, he told me, but it also serves as a barometer of the nature of a relationship. Unsatisfactory sex is going to cause it to bulge and burst somewhere along the line, like an aneurism.

But he has found that sexual dissatisfaction, alone, plays less of a role in marriage breakdown than is generally believed and that social class is an important factor. Sexual fulfillment means more in the upper class while emotional factors are important for the middle class. Finances and violence are the realities of the lower class. At the Marriage Council, Dr. Lief has found that sexual complaints, such as lack of feeling or agreement about sexual behavior, are the consequence rather than the cause of marital conflicts with three out of four couples. It is a vicious circle, but the root of a sexual problem can often be found in arguments about children, in-laws, money, or lack of nonsexual intimacy and communication.

The major problem Dr. Lief deals with in relationships is the undue expectations of people who place too much value on sexual performance and believe sex will remain as exciting as it was in the early days of the romance. "We seem to be a sex-obsessed society. There is decreased concern with the community and much more concern with self and with hedonism. People frantically go from one to another. It is a search for magic. They want to live effortlessly without hard work or real self-examination."

But you cannot counteract this by a basic return to the old verities or values per se, although an upsurge in neoconservatism throughout North America suggests this is the answer sought by many. For example, openness and honesty are often upheld as the best policy these days, but Dr. Lief says there is always the question of the lesser evil. To be honest and confess an affair to a spouse can be hurtful and dangerous. To remain silent may be an expression of concern for the other person, and may be the greater good. He does not support the extremist view that would have either honesty or secrecy under all circumstances. A committed relationship has to be open but there are things that are better not revealed. Dr. Lief doesn't see how anyone can avoid this qualification.

While many couples might be willing to accept a low-grade sex life, admission of adultery is *the* crisis which cannot be overlooked or euphemized. Whether it ends in divorce depends on the underlying strengths and weaknesses of the relationship. Since adultery is frequently a crisis situation and more visible than chronic dissatisfaction, many psychiatrists justifiably believe that infidelity is more likely to destroy the marriage than sexual ennui.

The sexual revolution has provided many options for couples today. The last twenty years have seen a unique spectrum of shocks and adjustments not just for the older generation but for young people as well. Who is to say which one is most shocked when the mother doesn't say anything about the fact that her daughter is living with her boyfriend? But marriage is still the preferred life-style for more than 90 per cent of people. Most couples who live together eventually marry even when they consider themselves part of the counterculture. Psychiatrists see it as an innate, intense desire for commitment. Dr. Lief says human beings are natural pair bonders and there is a tremendous desire to have one person mean the most to you. It is a necessary and complex drive which involves emotional security, available sex, and companionship.

A theory that is by no means conclusive but which Dr. Lief is pursuing is that women with high levels of the male hormone testosterone are better at forming lasting relationships. All those traits which promote social intercourse—ambition, achievement, and drive—are higher in these women. The intriguing suggestion for him is that the ability to pair-bond may be biological as well as psychological.

Open marriage, or marriage that allows sex with outside partners, is one of the alternatives to traditional marriage and Dr. Lief, as well as many of his colleagues, has seen his share of such couples. Younger people in particular claim to have eliminated jealousy from their lives but he has observed little evidence of this. No matter how much they protest, young couples and old experience jealousy when an affair takes place. Dr. Alex Comfort, author of *The Joy of Sex,* said that people won't understand sexual jealousy in the twenty-first century. Ideally it would be great to be a completely loving person and not suffer a lessening of affection from your partner when you share yourself sexually, but Dr. Lief guesses that if it ever happens it will be closer to the twenty-fourth century. "I don't see any indication that jealousy is disappearing. There is a need for exclusive possession of the other partner. No one wants to be possessed but we all want to possess. Jealousy seems to be some sort of protective mechanism. The reaction can be completely distorted but when it is appropriate it is a warning signal."

He told of a student survey in which it was reported that most young people expect extramarital sex will be an issue in their relationships, but they had no idea how they will handle it. However, thousands of couples have survived adultery and continued to stay together for their very private reasons. "There is a greater acceptance of adultery among ordinary people [these days]," Dr. Lief explains. "It is not as devastating as it once was." Sometimes adultery is a cry for help, the last chance to find each other again. But if an affair goes on for years, Dr. Lief feels that it means the partner has fallen in love with his or her lover. He has also found that when a man who commits adultery is discovered and he gives up the other woman, it is often a very cold-blooded decision rather than a declaration of love for his wife. When a philanderer does his cost accounting, he usually realizes that breaking up his family is more of a trauma than losing his mistress. At the same time, Dr. Lief stresses that people can love more than one person at a time; to suggest otherwise is "baloney."

Statistics indicate that many people are looking outside the home for pleasure and/or meaning. More than one half of men and nearly one half of women do not keep their marriage vows. If it weren't for unequal social standards, Dr. Lief says just as many women as men would have affairs because, biologically, there is no difference in their appetites. There is also research suggesting that sexuality is enhanced by anxiety, and that's why affairs are so exciting to some people. There is also the reality that a husband and wife have to deal with the children and mortgage while the lovers are concerned only with their mutual pleasure. The variety increases the sense of excitement and there is also a subconscious element that they are struggling against parental authority. Dr. Lief says: "Most of us never lose the sense of gloating over the fact that we're doing something naughty."

Intimacy may be more difficult to achieve today because the expectations of people are so high. Some of the support systems, such as family, church, and community, have changed, so more demands are made on partners to satisfy many needs. Still, marriage is seen as the best arrangement for raising children and Dr. Lief is not pessimistic. A majority of people have at least an *emotional* commitment to one person they want to stay with forever. Monogamy should be upheld as the ideal and until something better comes along, he does not see marriage threatened as the prevailing life-style.

Dr. Lief's personal belief is that psychiatrists and marriage counselors could benefit society as a whole if they could persuade couples to accept premarital counseling. They should be made aware of the pitfalls that befall every married couple. He also thinks couples should go for counseling a year after marriage and after the birth of each child. Instead, people let their troubles multiply and usually see a professional when it's almost too late.

The Marriage Council of Philadelphia tends to see younger people than the statistical average for such services. About 42 per cent of clients fall between the ages of twenty-eight and thirty-two and the problem is usually "seven-year itch," a colloquial expression for a period of marital restlessness often experienced after seven years of marriage. This commonly described but little-researched phenomenon is most obvious in the middle class and is characterized by an increase in extramarital sex (or fantasies of it), thoughts of separation, and a change of life-style and general marital dissatisfaction without apparent causes.

The term "seven-year itch" points to the number of years after marriage at which men, and increasingly women, supposedly develop a wandering eye. Some studies have indicated that "happiness measures" in marriage show steadily declining marital satisfaction from the early years to a low point five to seven years later, a second low point after fifteen to seventeen years of marriage, and then a regular increase in marital happiness afterward.

Dr. Lief recognizes the same symptoms with what is called the age-thirty transition, a major stage in individual adult development around the age of thirty seemingly brought about by boredom with the partner or severe work pressures. But the age-thirty crises might involve more than this, since boredom is likely to set in after one or two years of marriage in any case and work pressures are usually standard for men throughout their twenties and thirties. The age-thirty crisis is largely significant because it is the *first* transition period during which *all* commitments, including marriage, come up for review at the same time.

The move toward therapy at the age-thirty crisis is usually made by the partner who is experiencing changes in self-image and his vision of the world and the future. "I'm a different person now with different needs" and "If I don't change now, I'll be stuck forever" are the frequently heard complaints. Although most of the research on transition periods has been based on men, women apparently go through the same kind of painful evaluation. Dr. Lief said that when couples learned that the age-thirty transition was a common and appropriate experience, they were often relieved. The partner who was not involved in the transition phase was generally able to react with increased patience and understanding. Such a transition period may lead to divorce but can also return the marriage to a stronger footing. Trial separations of brief duration are common for transition-phase couples and are a way of checking out fantasies of a different life-style. Dr. Lief neither encourages nor discourages them but feels they more often turn out to be a vacation from a spouse than a genuine learning experience.

Marital therapists do not yet have a systematic and formally agreed-upon classification of marriage relationships. But Dr. Lief and Dr. Ellen M. Berman reviewed four such classifications for examining married couples, in a paper written for the *American Journal of Psychiatry*.

Classification 1
Based on Rules for
Defining Power

1. The symmetrical relationship. This is a relationship between two people with the same types of behavior; both are expected to give and receive; both give and take or-

ders. This relationship minimizes differences between the two people. Partners are seen as having equal but similar role definitions and tend to mirror each other's behavior. Problems come from competition.

2. The complementary relationship. Two people exchange different types of behavior. In marriage this relationship is most often described as traditional. One member is seen as "one up" and the other as "one down." Differences are maximized and each member exchanges dissimilar but need-fulfilling behavior evoked by the other. Less competitive than other relationships, it is often highly workable especially when the "one-down" partner has some areas of control. It angers some people because of the implication that the "one-down" person is seen as inferior.

3. The parallel relationship. The spouses alternate between symmetrical and complementary relationships in changing situations. They may be supportive and competitive without fear. According to some experts, this is the most desirable relationship for our egalitarian culture.

Classification 2
By Parental Stage

In today's nuclear family, the inclusion of children tends to produce the principal disruption to marriage. Other groups infringe on the couple but not with the force of children. Child raising tends to be crucial in terms of difficulties for the couple and other researchers have classified them in four stages: before child rearing, early child rearing, adolescent children, and after the children leave home.

Classification 3
By Level of Intimacy

1. The conflict-habituated marriage. It is characterized by severe controls, tension, and conflict. The partners are

held together by a fear of aloneness and the pseudomastery of controlling while angering their partner.

2. The devitalized marriage. This marriage is characterized by infrequent expressions of dissatisfaction, probably because of separate activities and interests. While there are no overt conflicts, there is numbness, apathy, and a lack of zest. There are periods of companionship but the relationship exists because of children and legal and moral bonds.

3. The passive-congenial marriage. This marriage is pleasant and feels comfortable and adequate to both partners. There is a sharing of interests but no deep interaction. Social supports come from outside the marriage and interests are with other people. The partners tend to feel that everyone's marriage is like that and derive some genuine feeling of support from the structure of their relationships.

4. The vital marriage relationship. This is an exciting and rewarding relationship and is highly important to both partners in at least one area, such as child rearing or work. The partners work together in an enthusiastic manner and the individual partner is seen as indispensable to the pleasure of the activity. There may be some conflict, but basically the marriage is stable and emotionally rewarding.

5. The total marriage. This is similar to the vital marriage except that it is more multifaceted. All reinforcing activities are shared and the partner is seen as indispensable. This relationship is rare and can be precarious because of power conflicts.

Classification 4
By Personality Style and
Psychiatric Terminology

(Several research groups have independently proposed this system.)

1. The obsessive-compulsive husband and the hysterical wife.

This is a conflict between the detached husband and the demanding wife or the "cold-sick" man and the "love-sick" woman. This pattern involves a somewhat dependent, obsessive man who has difficulty in expressing his feelings and is often seen as the strong, silent type. He wants to do the right thing and picks a woman who is the stereotype of femininity. She appears to be passive and somewhat seductive and has a marked tendency toward dramatic self-preservation. At first, she brings great excitement into her husband's life because she expresses and evokes feelings that he has never felt before. Taking care of her adds to his feelings of importance. On her part, she is looking for a good parent who will give her security. Once the couple experiences stress, the husband will regard his wife's more intuitive emotional nature and her analogical form of thinking as unpleasant and disorganized, and his wife will find his reactive emotional distance very disturbing. As she increases her nagging and he becomes more detached, each blames the other. It tends to be a parent-child interaction and may degenerate from the good parent with the good child to the distant parent with an angry child. Conflicts over intimacy become the central focus.

2. The passive-dependent husband and the dominant wife. The husband is originally attracted to a self-reliant woman in order to incorporate her strength. Because of his lack of self-assertion he feels inadequate: in addition, he may be alcoholic or obese. He handles his doubts about masculinity by choosing a woman who will take care of him. He usually picks a woman who has severe doubts about her feminine role and is uncomfortable in a dependent position and therefore chooses a man she can control. When conflicts arise, it will be due to the husband's increasing passive-aggressive behavior and depression, a reaction to his wife's attempts at overcontrol. Her inability

to dominate him and the frustration of her own unconscious dependency needs may make her angry and hostile. Power is the central theme.

3. The paranoid husband and the depression-prone wife. This relationship often has significant sadomasochistic elements. The husband, a jealous, suspicious, hostile, and angry man with concerns about his masculinity, may pick a woman who has low self-esteem and readily accepts blame. She's convinced she can do no better. Her low esteem can often be traced to excessively critical parents. She may choose a husband who is a psychological replica of the more rejecting parent and from him seek the approval that wasn't obtainable from the idealized and unreachable parent. These marriages are particularly stormy because both partners have inadequate coping and defense mechanisms and low self-esteem. Conflicts are almost always multidimensional.

4. The depression-prone husband and the paranoid wife. This relationship is the reverse of type 3. A woman who is suspicious and jealous marries a man who tends to be depressed and distraught. In addition to the masochistic elements in the husband's personality that permit the continuation of the painful relationship, the wife's suspicious and hostile nature gives the man the excuse for not moving into the outside world, which is too threatening. Conflicts often center around enlarging the marital boundaries to include others in their lives.

5. The oral-dependent relationship. Both members are passive, dependent, immature, and rivalrous. They both have intense longing for affection and feel they give more than they get. These relationships are very stormy, although occasionally the partners may be able to take care of each other. Both have temper tantrums and a desire for childish gratifications. Neither can show interest in the well-being of the other. The conflicts can be of any nature.

6. The neurotic wife and the omnipotent husband. In this relationship the woman is helpless and chronically ill and expects her mate to be omnipotent and relieve her suffering. She expresses unconscious resentment through depression and exaggerating her symptoms. The husband stays in the marriage because he wants to help and because of his extreme sense of inadequacy. He is strengthened by the idea of helping someone who is weaker but his continual failure results in loss of confidence. Power is the major area of conflict.

Dr. Lief and Dr. Berman point out that these marital styles do not always result in severe conflict and divorce. These couples find each other because of some kind of neurotic balance and if they are moderately flexible and have recourse to other patterns of behavior, the marriage can go rather well. Problems arise when one spouse changes or when he or she is no longer willing to live by the "rules."

Psychiatrists and marriage counselors have become involved in two complex and related phenomena: the rising divorce rate and the search for alternative life-styles. The controversy arises from the question of whether the divorces stem from the new sets of social and marital stresses common to the late twentieth century, or whether they are new solutions to old problems. In the opinion of Dr. Lief and Dr. Berman, the rising divorce and remarriage rates and the increase in marriage styles (i.e., open marriage) are basically a reaction to increased expectations and demands for happiness, autonomy, and the new experiences that were common during the nineteen-sixties. Some researchers see the rise in open contracts and serial monogamy as essentially normal and healthy responses to longer lives and urban life-styles. They predict an increase in the quantity and quality of these new experiments. But one thing is certain: psychiatrists' offices are filled with people who are alone, uncertain, anxious about whether to divorce, depressed after a divorce, or wondering about the need for more experience in life.

Couples come for treatment more readily than a decade ago but they are still very private about their marriages, according to Dr. James Miles, head of psychiatry at the University of British Columbia in Vancouver. More often it's the woman who initiates treatment. The core problem is that each partner feels betrayed by the other. They are unable to achieve intimacy; their needs aren't met; they feel unloved, misunderstood, and cheated. Sexual infidelity nearly always is a symptom of the underlying problems, and too often the problems result because they expected too much from each other. Marriage simply isn't what they thought it would be. Quite often they have married an illusion. If a couple is fortunate enough to have a good relationship they can withstand ordinary external stress and dissatisfactions, but looking at expectations from within causes the marriage to be severely tested, because it will often bring into focus past problems, perhaps even from childhood. Dr. Miles has found in his experience that marital problems can go back to the earliest relationships with parents. He says it's a poor start for a marriage when partners have little idea of each other's background.

Reduced to its simplest form, a person learns as a child about loving and whether it is safe to love. If attempts to love have been damaged at an early age, the adult will be leery and suspicious. Dr. Miles says, "I'll see a couple and one will be detached and the other is warm and loving and wanting closeness. With therapy the detached person can become warmer but then the other starts to withdraw. If you look at both their histories, he will have some reason to avoid intimacy and she has married a detached person so she can continue to appear to be loving without having to experience it. Everyone wants to be loved and nurtured and if you are handicapped in this area, inevitably it goes back to family history."

Dr. Miles sees mostly middle-class clients but he says economic levels don't affect the type of problem. He tries to change the way the individual sees himself and others. People reveal their natures and problems daily in picayune ways. For example, one wife explained to him that she was making french fries and her husband came into the kitchen and took over. They turned out perfectly. She was resentful while he insisted he was only trying to help. "What he was really doing was controlling her. He had developed enormous insecurity when his parents were divorced and the only time he could be comfortable was when he was in control. She had developed very low self-esteem and saw his rigidity as strength. I had to point out to him that he was a controlling and difficult person and I had to show her lack of assertion. I told her someone can only do to you what you permit. I had to change the way the couple expresses themselves. The truth of their relationship was that one of them had to control and the other needed to be controlled."

When couples come to him for therapy they are usually very angry and generally express it with sarcasm. He says getting the anger out of the way is relatively easy, but it's much more difficult to teach them to be tender. He doesn't see his clients at their worst. He says they've usually hit bottom and are trying to work their way up. The common motivation is to make the marriage better, but occasionally partners come simply to end their relationships without conflict: they want to be able to say they tried their best.

Some marriages that seem horrendous to him remain intact for their own "good" reasons. The partners are extremely dependent and for them a bad relationship is better than none at all. Some of the couples have been fighting since the honeymoon and wouldn't have it any other way. He says 10 to 15 per cent of his clients eventually divorce. That's as it should be for the sanity of some people, but he has little use for the stop-gap measure of a separation along the way to the end. "When they separate they say it's a trial to get their heads together. Often it's a chance to slither away without the moment of truth. Generally it is not an optimistic sign. If that's the only option they think they have, it's ominous."

Dr. Miles' personal feeling is that it's acceptable for some people to live together rather than marry. These people are more comfortable without a legal commitment and are more able to be intimate in a situation they feel they can walk out of if they want. Marriage is too intensive and constraining. They see it as a pressure cooker. But for most of us marriage is life's greatest endeavor and it has to be worked at constantly. Dr. Miles suspects that many physical ailments, such as flu, headache, and lower back pain, can be manifestations of the failure to achieve a satisfying relationship. He also considers marriage the only major step for which people are totally unprepared, except for the good and bad cues they picked up at home. Despite their lack of formal preparation, Dr. Miles is impressed by the intuitive powers of some people. "I have developed a deep and sincere respect for how people manage their relationships. Many have come from backgrounds that have ill prepared them to live with *anyone*."

The payoff in marriage is in direct proportion to what you put into it and that accounts for his clients who show up with nothing terribly wrong or right about themselves. They've stopped working at marriage and it has become a half life. But as long as the assets outweigh the liabilities, people will stay married. They don't split until there is a major imbalance. A human enough explanation is that most people don't want "the unmitigated hell of divorce." But Dr. Miles sees changes in society that are now contributing to marriages that are based on something more solid than this. Women's liberation was long overdue and it will have a positive influence on relationships when the wife is an equal, not a kept woman. Any movement in society that benefits the family has the greater likelihood of contributing to the growth of good relationships, and Dr. Miles says groups aimed at improving parenting are especially vital. His voice rising in volume, he says: "People are starting to realize how *goddamn* important it is to be a mother."

Dr. Gerry Erickson was director of the psychological service center at the University of Manitoba in Winnipeg when I met him. In contrast to Dr. Miles, he believes that "eight and a half out of ten people" he sees in therapy break up anyway. My immediate reaction was that this was a very cynical man, but he explained that his therapeutic goals have changed drastically in the past few years. He now defines success as facilitating a reasonable parting because it is impossible to keep so many of the couples he sees together. Some of them are interested in maintaining their marriages but more often one partner, usually the man, is looking for a way out. Dr. Erickson is amazed at how long people will allow themselves to remain miserable and unhappy. He spoke of a good friend who left his wife and five children after thirty-five years and who admitted afterward that he had serious concerns about the marriage after the first five years.

He says: "I don't know why some people suddenly start looking askance at their marriage but once they get into that kind of meditation they are bound to find something wrong, and I predict the end of the marriage in one or two years. Those who become dissatisfied and start scrutinizing their marriage are really scrutinizing their own ego. When I came to this university in 1969, there were some humanistic psychologists who were totally absorbed with the question of 'What about me? How am I doing?' but I have never taken that approach seriously." These are the concerns, perhaps the luxuries, of the middle class, he says. The poor and the black people he sees don't ask who they are. Instead, Dr. Erickson is face to face with a woman who hasn't left her house for four years and a husband who never comes home.

Dr. Erickson believes that if there is one thing that destroys a relationship, it's infidelity. The vitality of a person is crushed by this knowledge. He doesn't know why people confess to it except as a form of revenge. "I've seen a lot of middle-class couples who can talk of freedom of action and relationships outside marriage but to me that is a prelude to disaster. People can put up with a lot of other things but it is difficult to cope with someone who has been unfaithful. Almost everyone holds this value." He says a small percentage seem able to learn from the experience and stay together, but it always comes back to haunt them. He doesn't think it impossible for men to be faithful; acting otherwise is usually their way of saying they're sexually dynamic—as if that's all life is about. He abhors the idea that pleasure is paramount and everything else can go by the boards. Fidelity means honesty and trust, and people can occupy satisfying and separate worlds as long as they share mutual goals. Fidelity shouldn't be all that difficult to achieve, he says, but more people today view themselves as failures. It has become customary for some men to leave their wives after ten or fifteen years and they stand out as very poor examples for other men to follow. Dr. Erickson says if they get divorced for trivial reasons then getting married was obviously frivolous too. "They're the types who say at twenty-five, 'I'm in love and I should get married.' Then they get divorced like changing their socks."

Dr. Erickson says the family is not going to disappear; in fact, it's not even in any particular danger. There is a strong boundary around the nuclear family and it's hard to penetrate. Family experts are only beginning to learn what goes on. Dr. Erickson treats families as a unit and it's an improvement to finally deal with the family as a whole rather than sit alone with a child who stole six cars and try to understand what went wrong.

There is a strong feeling of malaise among the middle class, he says, and the tendency is to focus it on marriage. People don't seem to blame their own faulty ideas or their own personalities. No, *everything* can be blamed on the marriage.

It is discouraging to him to observe the rise in alcoholism and the number of women who take Valium. Sometimes he wonders if the ethos of today isn't more concerned with the value of real estate than the value of a strong system of belief. During times when everything looks so bad, I asked Dr. Erickson, why do people try to stay together? He didn't offer a psychiatric response, but spoke of the way he tends to handle it personally: "I never question my twenty-year marriage, which is a healthy thing. As far as I'm concerned, that's it. Trying to imagine splitting and a courtship period with someone else is ridiculous. Once is enough and I am satisfied. I wonder how people can tear themselves loose like that and leave their wives and kids. But I recognize that there are some rotten relationships and it's better that they get out of them and be different people."

There are people who run away thinking they'll never have to look over their shoulders. I think of a story I heard from a friend as we sat at an outdoor café in Montreal. A friend of hers discovered her husband's adultery and immediately walked out the door and sued for divorce. They never communicated again except through lawyers. Her former husband married the other woman and she took a lover. Years later, she deeply regrets that she never faced him, never allowed herself to talk it out. She still loves him and told my friend, "I'll spend the rest of my life wondering what if. . . ." These things happen when people are too self-centered and will do anything to avoid pain. "The nineteen-sixties was a period of great affluence in terms of money and emotions," Dr. Erickson says. "People's expectations rose incredibly and I think they were blind to the limitations. They seized freedom without any thought."

Dr. Harry Prosen, former head of psychiatry at the University of Manitoba in Winnipeg, has devoted a large part of his research to the crisis of middle age for men. It can have elements of adultery but it is more a time of generalized pain for both partners. It is a crisis that seriously affects the stability of a relationship, but as more is known and as it becomes recognized as a normal developmental stage, it does not have to be a devastating experience. The middle-life crisis, or climacteric, appears in many men somewhere between thirty-five and fifty and it can be the most devastating experience of all. Until around his fortieth birthday, a man has largely escaped the horror of self-definition by distracting himself with vigorous physical, social, and career activities. Now he has reached the plateau and faces the painful reality that he may not accomplish a great deal more; he is a mere mortal.

While the female menopause has been thoroughly researched, it is only recently that scientists have focused on the male middle years. Menopause is caused by the often dramatic lowering of the female hormone estrogen, and women know what to expect; they make at least a minimal emotional adjustment to the inevitability of aging and the loss of the reproductive function. But men have never been prepared for this because only rarely is there a male physical equivalent to the menopause. A gradual slowdown in the production of the male hormone testosterone plays a role in middle age but it is not sufficient to interfere with sexual activity or cause impotence—the great fear of middle-aged men—until well into the sixties and seventies, and often not then. The midlife crisis, doctors say, is mainly in men's minds but the anguish is real enough to produce physical and mental symptoms that seriously affect about 30 per cent of men, and are experienced to some degree by at least half of the men in the age group of forty to fifty. It often manifests itself in excessive work, affairs with other women, worries about virility, and noticeable changes in habits and personality. Even when the middle years produce only a low-grade psychological fever, wives sometimes find themselves stuck with an irritable, uncommunicative stranger who isn't too interested in sex anymore, at least not with them.

Dr. Prosen and his colleagues have been studying middle-aged men who conduct ongoing searches for women to love, often abandoning their wives and yet seldom finding what they seek. They usually cannot explain what drives them in their search. This type of man has been relatively happily married until he reaches middle age. His premarital dating record and sexual activity was sparse and his wife was often his first choice. He becomes dissatisfied with her and it may be expressed in terms of her aging appearance or in the complaint that she doesn't respond to his sexual needs. This results in the search for the other woman.

Dr. Prosen spoke of a forty-five-year-old teacher who married at twenty-three and had three children. His upbringing was middle-class and his parents had been isolated and unaffectionate. He tended to isolate himself as well and devoted himself to intellectual pursuits. His wife admired this and worked with him during the early years of his academic career. Although she never denied him, she didn't particularly enjoy sex. After becoming very successful, he met a younger woman who was from a completely different background but who was, like him, intellectual and opinionated. They developed a passionate sexual relationship and he left his wife after goading her and humiliating her to the point where she could no longer tolerate being with him. Dr. Prosen feels the experience is common among some middle-aged men.

One explanation is that the wife begins to look less attractive to her husband, while he usually continues to retain a youthful image of himself. In addition, he has his career and material possessions to enhance his self-esteem. But the human propensity to enjoy youth and beauty is not sufficient explanation for the search these men make. Dr. Prosen's theory is that as the wife ages, she seems physically more like the husband's aged mother. Since the strong reaction of the man as a young male to his mother was to an erotically interesting woman in her twenties or thirties, the fifty-year-old wife is no longer an appropriate mother substitute. "In his search for a younger and more attractive woman than his wife, a man may well be searching for the fantasized erotic mother of his childhood. He must attempt to discard his wife, who has become for him too much like the mother of his recent memory."

In these men Dr. Prosen has found a regression to earlier concerns about physical adequacy, masculinity, and success and there is often a need to reaccomplish the tasks of adolescence. There is a sense of ambivalence about his life and sometimes a desire to give up what he is doing and look for some new horizon to conquer. "In the finding of a narcissistically gratifying younger woman, the man gains attention and reaffirmation of his ability to attain a love object." Particularly for the man who did not experience sexual conquest in adolescence, the need to finally do so becomes urgent.

Other researchers have pointed out that an older man who takes up extramarital dating is enjoying the comfort of behavior already learned and is avoiding the pain, responsibilities, and adjustments of moving into the new developmental stage of the male adult life cycle. Apart from psychological and emotional stress in middle age, some men find themselves experiencing vague pains, lassitude, and a feeling of tiredness. The mental and emotional systems are insomnia, memory lapses, fearfulness, frustration, nervousness, irritability, even crying. A waning in sexual activity and a loss of self-confidence are directly tied in with the notion that his wife is no longer interesting and his job isn't satisfying. Something is dreadfully hollow and it's the rare man who wants to look within and ponder how much he might be to blame. To compromise his life's goals or admit that they are unattainable is to tamper with his essence, his carefully wrought self-image.

Raymond Hull, a Vancouver author and teacher, had most of these symptoms for two years when he was in his midfifties and he thought he was going mad. He told me that until the summer of 1968 he was in prime physical condition and then he began having what he called his "spells." He had desperate fears, wasn't able to think clearly, and couldn't get on with his work. He was critical of himself, his friends, life in general. He would often feel feverish, then in the next few hours be bitterly cold. One weekend he faced the cruelest fact of all, when an attractive woman friend showed up at his home unexpectedly—and slept alone. His sex drive had run out on him. Hull, a bachelor, diagnosed himself as having a full-blown case of the male climacteric. To keep in touch with himself, he started a diary of his symptoms. This was one of his entries: "Why didn't I go and see a doctor? By the time I set an appointment, the symptoms will have passed off, and I shall feel like a fool. Anyway, as soon as each spell is over, I feel fine, physically, emotionally and mentally—so I think there won't be another spell. Then, in a few weeks it starts all over again." With patience, exercise, and an increase in the amount of vitamins he had taken most of his life, Hull gradually recovered and went on to coauthor a book, called *The Male Climacteric,* with Dr. Helmut Ruebsaat of Vancouver.

Most troublesome of all, especially for wives who bear the brunt of it, is psychological instability during the midlife crisis. Harvard Medical School psychiatrist Thomas P. Hackett found men act in one of the following ways:

1. The Gauguin Syndrome. He is suddenly aware that he has never done the things he wanted to and pulls up stakes and goes after adventure, sexual and otherwise, before he's too old.

2. The Scapegoat-Wife Syndrome. Rather than examine himself when he begins to feel depressed or unfulfilled, he blames his wife for all his troubles and becomes critical and accusing.

3. The Sacred Amulet Syndrome. Very proud of his sexual potency, and now pained as it diminishes, he searches for a younger woman who can restore his virility overnight.

According to Dr. Hackett, there are three categories of

men who seem more immune to these syndromes: men who married late in life, including those who divorce and marry again; men who have first marriages that work, because they're either still deeply fond of their wives or have worked out practical methods of living together; men who derive great satisfaction from some other part of their lives, such as work, and are able to endure a poor marriage because it really isn't that important. It's the man who feels cheated by both his job and his wife who may be heading for catastrophe.

In order to deal with whatever stresses we have in keeping our relationships alive, Dr. Prosen emphasizes the importance of taking pleasure in whatever we do. Too many people think they can endure a lousy job and go away on holiday and something will change magically. Work and leisure have to be structured within our daily lives so that we do not find ourselves living by rote and drifting into some meaningless slough.

There are mother-father components in marriage and Dr. Prosen believes that it is essential to have both nurturing and dependency in a good relationship. As long as people are living together, there is not too much duplication of their original family conflicts. But once married, the original structure with its unresolved problems is usually revealed. He saw this with a young man whose mother had always controlled him. He tolerated the freedom of the career woman he lived with just fine until he married her. Then the neurotic depths were reached. Now he wanted to possess her just as he had been possessed. People who are newly in love aren't capable of or interested in closely examining the families of their future spouses. But it could give them a glimpse of what to expect a little farther down the road. The many stories, like that of the woman who cries too late that she should have known her husband's mother would never let him out of her clutches, are all too familiar.

It is a very human foible to think that we will totally remove ourselves from the influences of our parents and that we will never raise our children the same way. I can remember a friend telling me how disillusioned she was just two years after marriage and how she poured out her miseries to her mother-in-law. What she dared not say was that her husband had turned out to be exactly like his father, whom she could barely tolerate. Her mother-in-law said it for her: "I wanted to take you aside when you were engaged but I just didn't know if I should assume this responsibility. I wanted to tell you that you were marrying the same man I did. He's a bully and selfish and he will do everything he can to keep you under his thumb." The mother-in-law had developed a sense of humor and a deaf ear and waited for her husband to age and mellow, which he did to some extent.

The professionals told me that many young people marrying today are still unrealistic and fantasize under the spell of being in love. Try to tell them that love that endures is based on compatibility, security, and fondness, and the words fall on deaf ears. This is something you settle for when you're old and the thrill is gone.

Dr. Prosen speaks of the repetition compulsion. "We see people end their first marriage and already they're into a second relationship that will end as badly. There is no growth or change. When marriage breaks down, it's best to have an interlude and an opportunity to examine all the neurotic reasons for the breakdown. It's amazing how many people pick the same type of second partner and hope they will work it out. They are still too immature to handle a relationship." As a psychotherapist, his concern is to focus on establishing communication between the partners. It is important for them to understand that they have brought individual conflicts and repetition compulsions into their relationship. He often treads on dangerous ground because insights into one's vulnerabilities can hurt. His message is that a couple have to learn to work together with a sense of pleasure in everything they do including sex.

It's rare that sex is not an aspect of an overall marital

problem. Women's liberation has brought along some new twists. Women are demanding more from sex, especially in their middle age. Dr. Prosen calls this a new putdown for men. Women are making their needs known loudly and clearly and one of the current theories is that if women were allowed the full expression of their sexuality there wouldn't be civilization as we know it because they would require so many male partners. Prosen says monogamy was created for probably just this reason. He doesn't know if there is any physiological basis for monogamy but he does know that no openly promiscuous relationship he has seen has lasted.

In the homes of the couples I interviewed and in the offices of the psychiatrists and marriage counselors, the overriding concern in this age of transition has been the question of adultery. Do we continue to consider it the greatest sin and major cause of marital breakdown, or do we try to isolate it as a pure physical and pleasurable act which doesn't have to cause harm to anyone? Dr. Richard Wasserstrom, former dean of law and philosophy at the University of California at Los Angeles, has addressed this issue of whether adultery is immoral. He has no unequivocal answer but says if society is going to continue to change as rapidly as it has done, it's an ethical issue we must face sometime.

One argument for the immorality of adultery is that it involves the breaking of a promise which each spouse expects the other to keep. This breaking of the promise can be seen as an enormous indifference to the other person's feelings. A spouse may also see the act of sexual intercourse as a sign of affection for a third party. These are reasons enough to argue for its immorality but Dr. Wasserstrom also suggests that adultery always involves deception, and because deception is wrong it is to be condemned on that basis. Conventional sexual morality holds that intercourse is associated with the kind of affection for and commitment to another that is characteristic of the marriage relationship; it is natural that sexual intercourse should take place only between persons who are married. The traditional theory argues that feelings of affection that ought to accompany any act of sex can be held toward only one person at any given time. If that is so then the adulterous person is always committing an act of deception—either against his or her spouse or his or her lover.

However, Dr. Wasserstrom says whether or not adultery implies deception about feelings depends on the persons who are involved and the way they look at the meaning of sexual intimacy. He wonders if sexual intimacy should carry the burden of such exclusive promises and grave consequences. It may be that the enjoyment of sex for its own sake might do substantially more good than harm. Sex is an intense, exciting activity that can be enjoyed in a variety of settings with a variety of suitable partners. The situation, Dr. Wasserstrom suggests, may be no more different from that of a person who knows and appreciates fine food and who can have a satisfying meal in any number of good restaurants with any number of congenial companions. The question is whether we would gain or lose in a world where sex was no more or less significant than a good meal with a friend.

Another viewpoint in support of adultery as moral is that it is not the link between sex and love that needs to be broken but the connection between love and sexual exclusivity. Dr. Wasserstrom says the mistake lies in thinking that any "normal" adult will have these feelings toward only one other person. He suggests it is the concept of adult love, not ideas about sex, that need demystification. Some views hold it to be both unrealistic and unfortunate that exclusivity and possessiveness are the dominant factors of love. In the case of open marriage where couples agree in advance that extramarital sex is—in certain circumstances—acceptable behavior and there is no hiding of feelings about the other partner, adultery is simply not immoral, according to Dr. Wasserstrom. "At the minimum, adultery cannot very plausibly be condemned either on the grounds that it involves deception or that it requires the breaking of a promise." He says bluntly that a commitment to sexual exclusivity is not a condition of a marital relationship.

Along with the options and the desire for alternative ways of living in today's society, there ought also to be reasons for believing that marriage is a morally desirable and just social institution. The question of immorality aside, the strongest argument against extramarital affairs is that fidelity helps maintain the traditional nuclear family, which is ideally loving and healthy. But now there may be all sorts of intimate relationships which resemble but are not identical to the typical marriage, and these different sexual and loving arrangements may all legitimately claim to be called marriages, according to Dr. Wasserstrom.

So while our traditional morality may be effective in maintaining marriages that choose to be traditional, it is ineffectual in promoting and preserving others which are equally healthy but different.

This is the dilemma of Dr. Wasserstrom and the other psychiatrists and marriage counselors I talked to. At a time when every value is held under a microscope and subjected to the most intense questioning and doubts, it is no wonder that the professionals who would like to advise us are sometimes just as short of answers as the people seeking their help.

2

Honoring the Vows
Monogamy

Richard, thirty, and Marlene, twenty-six, were almost hailed as a media event when they pronounced in a Toronto newspaper interview that they were sexually faithful after one year of marriage and intended to stay that way. The newspaper was probing a suspicion that fidelity was back in style. The point is it never went away. For an awful lot of their readers this wasn't news; this was reality.

Richard told the interviewer: "If I were to feel attracted to another woman—I know it sounds right out of the nineteenth century—I'd admire her from afar. I guess there's nothing wrong with feeling the attraction. It's what you do about it that counts."

They're young in their commitment but they are repeating what generations of couples have promised each other. The difference in the last decade is that more people have made a practice run at commitments and promises by living together or having a series of partners. But after all the experimentation, most of them have wound up "married," whether they were churched or not, because couples who want to stay together don't want to share their bodies with the neighborhood.

Love seems to be becoming more exclusive once again and inevitably society is going to head toward some form of monogamy in the years ahead. An acquaintance of mine, who has settled into a monogamous relationship after years of affairs, confided: "I always did believe in fidelity but you have to be mature for it."

Perhaps elements of culture, religion, lack of initiative or opportunity, combine to keep some partners faithful to each other, but these days many more couples are eagerly and willingly entering into a monogamous relationship because of the acquired knowledge that we need the reaction of a trusted other person to know if we are *real*. These are the stories of some of the faithful.

Mona and Fred live in the capital of Canada, Ottawa, a civil service city marked by the occasional political scandal to entertain an otherwise ordinary population composed of a large number of temporarily posted residents. Although Ottawa is the fountainhead of political decisions, the reverberations are felt more strongly elsewhere. Generally speaking, the place is tight and provincial. Fred, as a lifelong civil servant and politician (he is a Member of Parliament), is very much a part of this insular world. At fifty-eight, he is two years younger than his wife. They have been married thirty-five years and have grown children and grandchildren.

Fred is highly respected by his colleagues for his intellect and absolute loyalty and reliability. There isn't in this man a hint of vicious rivalry or political background dealing. He neither creates nor seeks headlines, and outside his own political riding in Ottawa is unlikely ever to be well known. He is a quiet gentleman of the old school and only his wife is privy to his desires and feelings; he graciously refused to discuss with me whether his years of accomplishment, mostly unheralded, had been sufficient, or if he harbors resentment that his career has brought him no fame.

Fred's constituents like him for his dignified presence and his lack of artifice. He is white-haired and trim for his age and his equally handsome wife matches him perfectly in manners and decorum. But there is a difference because Mona laughs easily and he does not, and his controlled, chiseled face is rather disconcerting. Mona often tries to tease him out of his serious, aloof behavior and this is an asset as they make their rounds of the riding meetings, shaking hands and listening to the mundane problems which are all necessary to the process of being elected one more time. They're a team and the older voters always make a point of asking about her when Mona isn't by his side. Often, Mona, who is a housewife and mother, feels she's being elected along with Fred.

Our first meeting was in the restaurant of the House of Parliament, and with little consultation Fred ordered dinner for both his wife and me. Most of the conversation and the insights came from Mona, with Fred evaluating the questions and looking somewhat foreboding. She emphasized that theirs is a traditional marriage, as are those of their two children. She said there are enough problems in the world without trying to live outside the accepted norms of society. Their lives are literally lived as one. She is governed by a sense of loyalty and duty and she has been by Fred's side every step of the way. Whatever aspirations or potential talents she had were turned over entirely to his service. She was convinced of his brilliance and it seemed natural that she should do everything to make sure he achieved what he wanted. Not all political wives feel the same and Mona acknowledged this, but she was "astounded" by such women. It was perfectly natural for her, when Fred was running for office the first time and his campaign was lagging, to pick up their three-year-old child and go knocking on doors. She has never taken a break from campaigning for him.

Mona was an only child, born of early settlers on the prairies. When her mother died she was brought up by two aunts whose idea of life for her was that she would teach school and live at home. She and Fred met as university students and although he was always saying he was going to be a politician, she thought it was a young man's dreams. After he served overseas, they were married and her aunts, who expected her to be *"their* future," refused to attend the wedding. I suspect Mona is far less acquiescent than she appears to be even though the conversation during our first interview doesn't support me. She says: "I had confidence in him and I expected he could provide for us. I didn't have any talent to contribute so I didn't think of a career. But I didn't feel I was just a housewife because he brought me into everything he did." She has always had more than enough to keep her busy; she types his speeches and reads all his reports. They have had few purely social activities since 1958, when he was first elected to office after having served behind the scenes as one of the faceless members of the huge civil service that dominates Ottawa. He has lost a few elections and the first time it was devastating, "as if someone had dropped him off a ladder." On another occasion after an election failure, he applied for a civil service job but was turned down. He was bitter and at loose ends but, fortunately, Mona came into an inheritance and was able to tide them over.

Mona's friendly expression becomes more animated as she remembers periods in their marriage that have nothing to do with politics. Even Fred's fixed expression relaxes when she remembers the time he was on a fellowship in the United States and they lived on a farm, picked wild strawberries and asparagus, and canned peas together. "It was lovely and idyllic," she says, and then her voice recedes somewhat. "Maybe sometimes things are better remembered than relived." Then he taught at an American university, their son was born, and they developed some very close friendships.

Once back in Canada, Fred's job as a civil servant still left time for friends and parties, but after he entered politics their social life dwindled, and Mona found herself sending out Christmas cards to five thousand potential supporters she had never heard of. Before they could afford a constituency office or employees to handle the complaints and requests for favors, she took telephone calls at home. "I spent a lot of time talking to people who wanted to blow off steam. I had to keep records of all these calls, but I didn't resent it. It used to be that when we went out for an evening I would try to write down the names of three potential supporters I might be meeting. My daughter-in-law was always saying to me, 'Why not take a university course and do something on your own?' But there is nothing I find as interesting as politics." Of course, if her husband were not the kind of man who confided in her, she says she might feel differently. As it is, when there are depressions in his life, she is there to soothe him with quiet conversations. She even goes fishing with him, something she never expected to do. She encouraged him to learn wood carving and he's turning out some exquisite pieces. Her role has been to keep the peace and to shore him up and, mother or not, it is not with equanimity that she tells me that her husband now confides all his business concerns to her son *the lawyer,* and not to her.

But if politics is interesting, it is far from joyful. It is full of conflicting emotions; you may wake up eager to do the tasks and full of accomplishment, or the hours and the people you deal with may be so exhausting that you go to bed thanking God for the invention of sleep, not for the rest that's in it but for the unconsciousness. Politics has taught Mona two things: you have to be with people you would never want to be with otherwise; and not too many marriages can withstand all the time spent apart. It is lonely and frustrating waiting for Fred to come home, and they have attended perhaps only three intimate dinners with friends in any given year. The only thing she can truly count on is Sunday dinner at home.

Fred finally enters the conversation. All through this precisely timed dinner, Mona has built up from pleasantries to more revealing statements and her husband has watched and said virtually nothing. I feel as if I have watched a two-character play in which one character spends the first two acts delineating the main character, who until now has looked wise and indicated by facial expression that his story has been told more or less correctly.

It wears him down, he says, that he usually works from seven-thirty in the morning to ten-thirty at night and that the weekends are never free. Social standards have changed considerably in the last ten years in Ottawa, he says, and the impression is that he is not pleased. He tells me an unmarried politician is not criticized if he has affairs. He turns to Mona: "I think we're pretty compatible and pretty lucky. It's a tough business but I can go home at night. We don't have the same domestic crises as other Members of Parliament because we live in our riding. It's hard for those men who have to decide whether to bring their families to Ottawa. But when their wives are here, I think their marriages have a better chance of surviving."

He speaks of his defeats at the polls. It wrecked his career, everything. It interrupted what he felt he had achieved. It hurt his self-confidence to wake up in the morning and realize that he was unemployed. It took him eighteen months to find a job he wanted. Politics also determined the size of their family, which is not without regret for him. Mona had several miscarriages and they wanted a large family. One of their three children is adopted and Fred wishes they had adopted more, but he accepts the situation gracefully. "Politics is my whole life and my hobby and it gives me tremendous satisfaction. I know someday I'll write a political book and I might go into business with my son, but I don't like to think of early retirement because this is wrong for me. I am fifty-eight years old and I have no intention of quitting."

Fred says he knew Mona would be a fine politician's wife because she has an even disposition. They share traditional values and he makes a point of the fact that there have been no divorces and that no one in the family smokes cigarettes. And that, he says, is because his children were never given an alternative. Mona has spoken of her husband's brilliance and he recites the facts. He was ten years old when he started high

school and had graduated from university while still a teenager. He was very shy and serious then, and has remained so.
He is very conservative and has no qualms about being perceived as such.

Nor does it bother Mona that some people would think
she is totally unliberated, too self-sacrificing, an unredeema-
ble relic from the past. She knows all about the opportunities
for freedom, but they offer her nothing. Both of them have
adhered to the old rules and are equally pleased. Fred says:
"I'm so conventional on so many fronts but I wouldn't change
any of it. I have a theory that we work out our own fates and
given other chances we're still not likely to act otherwise. I
have a job to do and a sense of purpose and achievement. I'm
not likely to be a cabinet minister. Had the throw of the dice
been different, I know I would have been. But I have status
and I don't swim with the tide. We faced bankruptcy one year
and for a few years politics and business seemed to be very
bad. But we worked our way through and now that strain isn't
there anymore. I was ready to throw in the towel in nineteen-
seventy-three but she wasn't. If Mona hadn't thought I had
more to contribute, I probably would have given up. Our children have a greater commitment to their country and a sense
of duty and we have a sense of commitment to our marriage.
It's a building commitment. It's not something that's going to
fly apart."

Mona thinks of all the years she had to keep the children
quiet so Fred could study and she thinks of the people who
say, "I'll work and you study and we'll put off having a family." The mutual goal seems to be zero population. That has a
lot to do with people's selfishness. If you're a mother you can't
be selfish too long, she says. If the husband is the breadwinner,
then the woman must play the supporting role. If both have
careers, whose career is more important? However, she admits
that discontent does crop up in trifling ways. Once in a while
she wonders why he can't do the dishes for a change. Sometimes she longs for a slight change in the domestic routine.

She is concerned about the effects of retirement on Fred. He'll need her companionship more than ever and "we'll get through it whenever it happens." Then there's that other eventual adjustment: Fred has been away from home so much during their marriage they've never had time to be bored with each other. What about being together too much? That's for later consideration, she says.

During my visit to her home, Mona was far more relaxed; in fact she was wearing her husband's socks and slippers. Two little grandchildren were tearing around the house and sunshine was pouring through the windows. It didn't seem as difficult to bring up the subject of sex and the politician now that we were alone. It's everywhere, she acknowledged, even for an older man. There are always women looking for adventure and a chance to see how power works. They don't care what they do to a man or his family.

All their married years, there was never a hint that Fred had been unfaithful, but a few years ago a ludicrous woman entered their lives and Mona is angry and bitter still. The woman started visiting his office, saying she was a constituent and becoming bolder in her behavior. She telephoned Mona and said Fred was giving his wood carvings to other women. Fred frequently had lunch with women and she had never thought about it twice. But to demonstrate the irrational power of suspicion, she actually found herself looking at his work schedule. "I found he had dined two times with a woman and I became very hostile. I just wasn't happy and he agreed he would not have dinner with a woman anymore, leaving me at home on the phone with a constituent watching the soup get cold." Their formerly peaceful lives were set on edge when the woman began telephoning at night and hanging up. She spread rumors that she was his mistress and mailed pictures of herself in suggestive poses. It ended as unexpectedly as it began, but not before Fred had to tell her bluntly: "I didn't have sex with that woman but I feel as dirty as if I had."

That's how much things have changed. It seems appalling

to Mona, who should be resting on the safe shoal of sixty years of age and decades of monogamous marriage, that she has to wonder if it could happen again, or if that next woman might be too attractive and irresistible. "In our day," Mona said, leaning toward me with a bewildered look that I have seen on the faces of so many different generations of women, "if you knew a man and a woman were together, you did *not* interfere!"

The interference that Emmerson, twenty-seven, and Lea, twenty-six, had to deal with was not sexual but racial. He is black and she is white and they have been living together faithfully for eight years, most of the time quite happily after the liberated sixties saw the beginning of much more racial tolerance. Some might ask what they are doing in a chapter on monogamy when the traditional definition means sexual fidelity to the person you've married. But the expanding times have broadened the term. Many marriage counselors and psychiatrists speak of monogamous relationships without making any distinction between married or unmarried people. Certainly, Emmerson and Lea consider their belief in and practice of faithfulness to be as valid as the next couple who might be married. Perhaps because they don't feel bound by any moral rules or a legal marriage document, they have found that faithfulness has been a natural outgrowth of their commitment to each other. They also believe they're more easygoing and have fewer problems with jealousy.

Emmerson was raised in Harlem and Lea comes from a comfortable Mideastern background. They met at an upperclass university, where he made it through on scholarships and the admonitions of a remarkable ghetto mother who told him from the time he was a child that he could do or be anything. She made it clear she would tolerate no racial excuses from him. Still, his mother and Lea's parents weren't overjoyed by their relationship. At first his mother and his friends said he was putting down black women. She describes her parents as "the usual liberals" which, translated, means that they invited Emmerson to the house but made him feel as awkward and uncomfortable as possible. But on the campus it was as easy as could be: being a mixed couple was almost a mark of liberation. Later on, Lea's parents accepted the situation.

Emmerson's life is committed to political action as a community organizer in black and Hispanic areas of New York. He wears conservative suits for his meetings with the power men at City Hall and wears his "dude" clothes on the streets, making sure people receive efficient garbage collection and getting the neighborhoods concerned about safe streets and what's happening to their kids in school. In a city as impossible as New York to govern, Emmerson's crusade is to build up one little neighborhood at a time. Lea is a journalist and believes passionately in Emmerson's causes, but compared to him she is nearly apolitical. They have a flat in a brownstone in a good area of Manhattan which they share with Lea's three cats.

Emmerson and Lea are openly affectionate with each other but are not reticent about disagreeing or questioning any opinion the other holds. They are not materialistic and what furniture they have is worn to the point of collapse, yet they couldn't care less. But it's a nice touch when Emmerson sets down two excellent bottles of Margaux and some wineglasses on the bare floor. He is handsome, always smiling, and some may think him a little ingratiating; I think he carries a healthy dose of self-parody that certain street pros can bring off very well. There is no question he can handle himself with equal grace with the hustlers in the alley and the hustlers in the anteroom of power. Lea is more aggressive in her gestures and facial expressions and is not overtly accommodating. She seems to present herself as a package: Here's my face—interesting but conventional; here's my body—very nice; and here are my opinions—straight up, take them or leave them. She is wary but kind. They're both amateur artists: her works are geometric pen-and-ink drawings and his are romantic landscapes in oil.

They tell me they have never had a conversation about their relationship with a stranger before. They know couples who sit down and talk about how they're doing all the time, but this was the first time they have put together a sequential story of their lives together. Getting up to execute a few dance steps, Emmerson announces: "We have stayed together this long because it has been *fun!* And as long as it's *fun* we're always going to stay together!" This, apparently, is monogamy, latter-day style.

"Marriage to me has a meaning that I can't accept right now," Lea says. "The main thing is the fearsome permanence. I much prefer to leave it open-ended. I feel as deep a commitment to Emmerson as if we were married but there is a relief in not being thoroughly enclosed. I might get married if I had a baby, or if I were eighty years old, or if I found myself succumbing to social pressures. I still have all the romantic ideas I was brought up with as a child and sometimes we have conversations about whether we should get married. I always end up saying, 'God, that's so scary!'" Life-style should be a matter of choice, she adds, but there seems to be a "fascist compulsion" to make everybody live the same.

Emmerson is not hardheaded about marriage. He wouldn't mind getting married but the important thing is that they enjoy each other. There's no point taking a chance on spoiling it. When people get married, this mechanized switch seems to go on and suddenly they start playing the role of *husband* and *wife*. "It just doesn't seem to have a happiness factor," he says. By contrast, they're so easygoing they don't feel they have to work at staying together. But there has been a significant change in their attitudes. During their first six years together, they lived on a day-to-day basis, not counting on their future. Now months pass at a stretch during which neither doubts that the other will be there.

Lea describes the two of them as very adaptable, patient,

loving, and accommodating. When she's in a bad mood, he tries to find out why. He doesn't get angry. Lea talks of commitment; Emmerson talks of love. He knew he loved her when he was given a scholarship to study languages in France and came back to New York after a few weeks because he couldn't bear being away from her. He was always a romantic who thought of finding one person to live with the rest of his life. Then, in one of those universal gestures made by couples who feel particularly warm and pleased with each other, they pulled out a scrapbook of pictures taken during those months of friendship before they realized they were in love. It might have been any of the wedding albums I had been asked to look at along the way. The pictures remind Lea of how she always thought of Emmerson as the man she wanted to be with, and never as the *black* man. The color of a person's skin is simply a difference in appearance, and no more than that. She tells Emmerson: "I was surprised at the power love exercises. I have no idea what I would be doing if it weren't for you." Emmerson acknowledges this with a warm smile and says something I suspect he has said many times before: "I sometimes do have this impulse to have children." Lea says she doesn't want to go through the physical changes of pregnancy and that she doesn't want that lifelong responsibility right now. "But it would be nice to shape a child, to give him opportunities, to turn him into a really nice person."

Emmerson says he is unequivocally faithful to Lea and depends on Lea to be faithful to him. That should be obvious, Lea says. "I feel a tremendous fidelity. It's partly a cohesiveness. Most successful relationships I see have a quality of being special. Sometimes that changes over from passion to companionship. We have this special feeling and if either of us strays, we will have lost it. I feel more than ever that sexual satisfaction and trust are crucial to keeping people together." However, if there were an affair she doesn't think it should mean the end of their relationship. "Oh, you think *not?*" Emmerson challenges. "I think you're committed enough to me that you would stay and try again," she answers. He says he would rather not deal with that situation at all and, turning to me, he asks: "If she had slept with someone else, how could I predict exactly what my behavior would be in one of the most traumatic situations of my life?" Lea explains this is precisely why they constantly check each other's feelings, why they don't let deep-rooted problems fester. Emmerson offers the opinion that open sexual relationships are a very cynical way of approaching life. "We're so lucky," he says. "Nothing drastic has happened to our faith in each other and our days of laughter are not over yet." Their generation still has many of the old values, Lea says, but the children coming up have too much too soon. "Sex is heavy and kids today aren't told enough for what they're getting into."

They have the usual disagreements and compromises of any married couple. She thinks he's messy and that she has to clean more. There are personal quirks and habits each has to tolerate without making too big a deal of it. They have separate savings accounts and insurance policies and the rest of the money is shared for household expenses. It should not matter but Lea feels less equal financially because Emmerson makes more money and pays for more. "But I'm fighting to maintain my equality. I certainly think that I'm as equal as you. I have an ego." Emmerson tells her it would be unhealthy for her *not* to have an ego. She thinks he's a little sexist; he doesn't agree. She confesses that although she considers herself a feminist, she hasn't done much to contribute to the movement. Lea also says that she can't quite get over the feeling that Emmerson's work is more important than hers. Look, he tells her, she is a good journalist and she is doing her part by getting out honest information. But there's more for her to do. He wants to see her become a great writer with some power. As for him, there's no question he's passionate about politics and could talk about it all night. He knows big government is hopeless and his work with the poor often seems in vain. People have been down so long that it takes a lot of persuading to convince them that it's a first step up if they begin by cleaning the garbage off their streets. "Sometimes I feel I'm having the greatest time playing games and sometimes it's dreadful, drilling pressure. I want to get really good at what I do. I want to make a mark on the community." There is a possibility that Emmerson will run for a public office and it's a major disturbance for Lea because she knows she will have to settle for less of his energy and passion. She realizes that he's aspiring to work for the greater good but she's selfish enough to want to keep a portion of him to herself.

They describe briefly how they were involved in the drugs and the radical movements of the early seventies and how everyone's consciousness was raised. It was fun, it was exciting, and it is gone. Their contemporaries woke up one day and found out that the revolution was over—and they weren't even sure if one damn thing had been accomplished. All around, they saw friendships dissolving in the light of that realization. But out of the debris of that particular decade, Lea and Emmerson say they managed to develop a way to stay together.

What Emmerson and Lea have learned is not so different from the lessons to be taken from the conventional marriage of Steve and Myra, who live a serene life in British Columbia. They are in their sixties and adhere to certain traditional moral values, though they were very aware of the sixties revolution and in many ways welcomed doing away with some rigid and unnecessary social rules of thirty years ago. They accept the fact that people don't necessarily marry and that this often works well for certain types of personalities. But they say society can't ignore monogamy entirely if it hopes it will last. While, like all the couples I interviewed who spoke of the importance of mutual respect and a sense of humor in a lasting relationship, Steve and Myra were the only ones to point out the importance of "good old-fashioned manners." Their manners are impeccable; they are gracious and charming, and they also prove that being polite and knowing how to behave correctly in social settings is not synonymous with being stiff and intimidating.

They live in a large elegant apartment predominated by Steve's studio and his paintings. Both are small and graceful in stature. Steve's hair is still brown and he is shy, old-world courtly, and deferential toward women. He chooses his words carefully and has a habit of reaching out and feeling the leaves of a nearby plant, as if in constant need of texture. Myra has lovely skin and youthfulness and can wear her gray hair and clothes in whatever current style pleases her. Their age has not relegated them to their own generation. Friends are older and younger, a few artists, some businessmen, and a great many writers; they are interested in the world of ideas. A West Coast acquaintance told me it was something of an honor to receive an invitation from them because they keep out of the public eye and prefer the intimacies of long-term friendships. There were many pauses between Steve's sentences but Myra kept smiling encouragement at me, as if to say the interview was going well and what I finally heard would be worthwhile.

Steve told me that he doesn't believe either of them was completely mature when they married, even though he was seven years older and both of them felt they had quite a bit of life's experience. He had come from Europe to British Columbia during the Second World War and met Myra on a blind date. That was the usual way for young people to get together in those days with so many of the local men being sent overseas. They were married within months and had no firm expectations for the future. "We wanted to get married and be happy," he says. "I know it sounds oversimplified but that's how it was." Because they did not expect their lives to proceed along a given path, there was no conflict at all when Steve announced, after seven years as a businessman, that he wanted to be an artist full time. He had studied painting in Europe and had worked at it in his spare time and Myra knew the day would come when he would have to find out how good he was, even though there would be no more regular paychecks. Steve and Myra believe it's inevitable that plans will change as you go through life and that's why marriage contracts, which some couples favor today, are totally unworkable. You can't put down in writing what your life will be in the future and you can't anticipate individual growth. "I think a marriage contract is a mark of insecurity and immaturity," Steve says. "You're saying, 'I expect you to look after me but if you do something wrong, I won't necessarily have to honor this contract.'" Besides, Myra adds, a lot of "luck" is involved in choosing a good partner.

Steve knows *he* was lucky. Any other woman would have made him feel guilty when he quit his job because it was disruptive and hard on Myra and their three small children. But she could see their way through. She had been trained as a laboratory technician and told him to take off two years, see what he could do, and she would worry about the finances. It meant a couple of "skinny" years, keeping the children quiet and listening to the annoying questions of people who would say, "Is he still painting?" as if what he was doing weren't *serious*. But this was better than living with a frustrated man who had been thwarted by circumstances from trying out his dream. What Steve accomplished was splendid. Today, he is regarded as one of the finest artists in Western Canada.

Steve says the real key is what a person can make of a relationship and not what he expects to get from it. Some people understandably resent ties that bind because they mean giving up total freedom, "but you gain a different freedom and someone with whom to share things." Even still, he adds, you don't share everything. He doesn't, for instance, discuss his work in progress with Myra because talking can dissipate the emotion involved. He definitely does not share his studio; when he is there he is completely unto himself. He works long hours during the week and a few hours on the weekend, and that is perfectly understood. It is sheer discipline; no serious artist waits around for inspiration to move him just as the serious marriage must recognize that there are no days when the duties and rewards of marriage are evenly split. Sometimes one person needs more and you should be willing to give it.

Myra believes that many marriages that break up after twenty-five years or more have not been basically good marriages. Often enough, they have been held together for the sake of children. There are gradual things that happen if you're not careful, such as simply growing apart. One day it seems there's nothing left to talk about, everything has been said. This wouldn't happen if people remained alive to what's going on in the world, if they understood that every day contains the capacity for surprise. After twenty-eight years constantly under the same roof, they have never faced any chasm of silence. Both have their outside lunches and gatherings, and when there is free time for each other they like to travel, take walks, listen to chamber music, and read. "But no life is without trauma," Myra adds. In the pause that follows this statement, I wait for Steve's reaction. (My West Coast acquaintance had told me that Myra recently came through a serious illness and that Steve had been devastated by it.) "You may say everything goes along pretty well," he tells Myra, "but you have been sick a lot." She brushes it off, saying how one copes with problems is all a matter of temperament, and hers is just fine.

She won't have a fuss made over her and changes the subject by saying that while they still adhere to traditional values, they are influenced by the changing times. Society in their day would not tolerate couples simply living together but now she feels that's nobody's business. Steve isn't so sure that getting rid of all the old taboos has made life easier. He objects when Myra says there is nothing one can do but accept changing standards. "This complete avoidance of judging people is going too far. You can't completely not make judgments. There have to be guidelines, especially for children. If there are no rules there is a great sense of insecurity." He feels men and women are equally capable of being monogamous, that there is nothing in a man's physical or emotional makeup that means it is more difficult for him. He finds it repulsive that a man would want to be intimately involved with more than one woman at a time. Myra agrees that affairs are a great cruelty but she can understand why some women would accept them. She has seen women divorce in anger and regret it. If an affair is going to blow over, some women—and men—feel it is better to endure than head into a lonely old life. They're grateful that their three children have solid, traditional marriages and they say this is because children reflect the attitudes of their parents. Since their marriage was happy, their children expected the same for themselves.

One of their guiding principles is that you have to be nicest to the person you live with. You have to accept that marriage, far from being a limiting experience, is the greatest learning and humanizing process. Only by becoming deeply entangled with another person can you discover the real demands and possibilities of human behavior. They believe it is only human nature to speculate how things might have turned out had they chosen a different mate. They say the lucky people are those who are glad they made the decisions they did.

I do not know of anyone who has had more time to reflect on the wisdom of his decisions than Dr. Tom, who was ninety-three years old and fifty-six years married when I met him. While his wife was fussing with her hair in the bathroom off the room they share in an old folks' home, he told me in a tone of voice that conveyed a great sense of victory: "We've done it! We've lived together all these years." There was a great deal of the learning and humanizing process of marriage behind that statement.

He was a little annoyed that his hearing aid hadn't arrived yet but he said it would work out—as had his whole life. His ninety-three years have been a continuum of small, private realities about which you became upset or you didn't. While he waited for Violet to appear, he sat in a green vinyl chair that matched hers nearby. The walker he used to get around the room and to the corridor beyond was identical to hers. He smiled. A child starts his life in a walker and a man ends his in one. As a doctor, he took care of people for fifty-two years. Now, nurses and doctors take care of him and lively West Indian nursing assistants pat him here and there. The closing of the circle of existence is realized for Dr. Tom in his Toronto home by the fact that in one glance he can take in all the objects they own in one hospital-sized room. His toiletries and hers. His clothes, among them the pink shirt and tie and beige cardigan he is wearing for the interview; her clothes, the ageless dresses with small white flowers on dark backgrounds. His medical journals and *her* telephone. The available space, an implicit order of things, is equally shared.

Violet, impossibly, wants to be active, to get outside and do those things she had done—surely not so long ago? She had always been contrary and she spoke her mind. He, however, had always been able to smile and walk away when she wanted to get into a row with him. *Patience.* He had been patient when he courted Violet for five years in the second decade of the century, meeting her on the country roads outside the town of Whitney, Ontario, and taking her on his medical rounds. He had patience now as he waited for her to come out of the bathroom, his slow-moving Violet with a new complaint about something—and his Violet of the roads. Both Violets were welcome. He had, after all, made a commitment to her for life.

Violet finally joins us and she looms larger than her short, slightly built husband, whom she calls, variously, Tommy, Dad, and the Doctor. She has a thick, curly head of white hair for her eighty-seven years and a comfortable, pleasing spread to her body. She's a lively talker, a woman used to running the show. She gave a lot of her life to the Women's Missionary Society and the Women's Christian Temperance

Union and for years she organized plays and took them
around to Ontario towns, especially around Woodbridge, a
community near Toronto, where they lived for thirty-three
years. But the doctor has certainly exerted his influence. Even
though she had taken the pledge never to drink and reached a
high level in the WCTU, he sometimes persuaded her to hoist a
few with him. Tommy, she says with a great deal of warmth,
still likes his alcohol. "My *booze*," he corrects her. The doctor
has this offhand manner and little audacities of speech that
some shy and sensitive men acquire when they have to deal
with all sorts of conditions and people.

Violet describes him as the last of the real country doctors. After graduating as a surgeon and general practitioner in
1914, he looked after the medical urgencies of six hundred
lumbermen in Northern Ontario. "My father was a lumber-
man and that's how I came to meet him," Violet says. "I was
just staying home and keeping my mum and dad company. I
didn't have to work. My dad gave me everything I wanted."
She suggests, coyly, that he took to her because she was the
only girl around. He says it was because "she just grew on me.
I can't say it was love at first sight because I never did jump to
conclusions. You have to satisfy yourself about what you're
getting, you know." She says: "There's nothing he can do
about it now, unless one of us dies. Certainly I'm not going to
die young. Nobody in my family died young." He answers:
"I've been married so long that I can stand anything. I'm
tough. I've worked the lumber and mining camps. I've practiced as a doctor in Saskatchewan, British Columbia, and Al-
berta. I've taught school and I've worked on the Canadian
Pacific boats."

Violet asks if he remembers how he had to go out nights
on a sleigh to his patients and got stuck in the snow so often.
"What I remember," he says, "is that they didn't pay for their
bills. All I got was their promises for pay. I was lucky if I
collected from half of them."

Back and forth their talk goes in no particular sequence,

picking out the highlights such as the birth of their only child, Shirley, who is an "angel," who looks after them, doing all the banking and mailing, getting the doctor's tobacco and alcohol. After a number of small-town medical practices, they settled in Woodbridge in an eleven-room house where the doctor had his office. "He'd leave the medicines out for his patients," Violet explains, "and I'd give them out and clean up after their dirty feet and answer the telephone." Constant sharing was the fabric of their lives. Violet tells one of her favorite anecdotes, which she says should show how she and Tommy get along. The doctor intuits which story she is going to tell and he nods in approval. Then he seems to turn off the hearing aid he doesn't yet possess. When Tommy was in the hospital with six broken ribs, Violet says, she came to pick him up and take him back to their Toronto apartment, where they lived for eleven years before moving into the nursing home. They had to give it up because of failing health. "Well, there he was kissing all the nurses good-bye," she says, "and with *me* right there! He had a whale of a time." The doctor drifts back in and mutters: "I hope she's getting that one right. I'm not sure that's the way it happened." Then he smiles slightly at her suggestion that he's a bit of a rascal at his ripe age.

"I've never been jealous, though," Violet adds. "I knew when I got married I'd never get rid of him. I don't think such a thing as a divorce ever came into our minds or that we had a big scrap at any time. I tried to but he'd just grin and walk away. Oh, sometimes I felt like boxing his ears but I never got around to it. I suppose he wanted to put me through a wringer more than once but he didn't." When the doctor leaves the room for a moment, his wife leans forward and whispers in a touching burst of enthusiasm: "Don't you think he's wonderful? That man still keeps up with foreign affairs and medicine and he knows about money matters. It feels wonderful to be together."

As the visit comes to a close, the doctor says that "too much freedom of thought" is the reason so many marriages break up. It's being too concerned with having your own way, being too unwilling to make a commitment and stick with it. "The secret of staying married so long," he says, "is forbearance and patience." He repeats the word *forbearance*, underlining it with his voice. His wife sits up in her chair and looks a little surprised. "Tommy, why are you looking at *me* like that?" When he doesn't answer, she asks where her shoehorn has gone. The doctor, very willingly, begins looking for it.

A man I know, who has turned forty and is beginning to think about aging, believes that the ability to love when you're older must come when you perceive reality only in the eyes of the other. You lose your selfishness day to day and you discover the absolute joy of being in the service of someone who has always been in yours. Your beloved is a mirror of your own reality and what you have left. I thanked him for this thought because I think this may be the essence of love stories that work.

3

Forgiving People
Compromise

Just as the unexamined life seems to hold less value for us than the life of experimentation, a marriage that has never been tested can become a lifeless caricature with all its endless possibilities left unexplored. Whatever form the challenge to any relationship takes, it will inevitably involve change, pain, and growth. Some marriages will end because of the stress; some will settle into a kind of unarticulated acquiescence and a desire to keep the peace at any cost; and others will move forward into new, firmer territory.

If infidelity is the challenge—and chances are it will be—there will be a lasting ache but it could become a departure point from which the couple can stand back and assess themselves, and perhaps come together again as stronger individuals.

During that time they may consider who they might have been with or what they might be doing otherwise, without their partners. They are forced to decide whether this is home base and if it is enough. I spoke at length to three people who tested their marriages to the limit, who faced reality, perhaps not gracefully, and who came to know the contours of themselves and their spouses. Each asked me not to interview their spouse, since the past is cruel to them and there are gaps better left unfilled for everyone. All three have remained with their spouses, not out of habit or lack of opportunity to go elsewhere, but because they now *know* where they want to be, and why. In each case, the test was adultery.

I didn't know what to think of Leslie, the legend, when I finally met her. She had been described to me in glowing terms by her ex-lover, Paul, who is an acquaintance of mine in Toronto. He told me she had been a charming companion in the fulfillment of many of his fantasies, and when he learned that I would be in New York City, he gave me her business telephone number and told me she would be an interesting person to talk to.

Leslie seemed a little startled when I called but quickly invited me to drop by her neighborhood bar. I arrived a little early and following Paul's instructions was on the lookout for an attractive, elegantly dressed woman in her fifties. I didn't want to make any prior judgments but I had told Paul I didn't particularly approve of extramarital relations and that checking out his former lover could prove embarrassing all around.

I was relieved to find that she was as nervous as I was and I liked the way she became instantly warm and personal. She spoke familiarly to the waiter about her usual drink, then turned her welcoming smile on me and looked directly into my eyes. "How do you know Paul?" she asked. I explained that I sometimes consult him on the phone about business matters. She accepted this and didn't probe for more details. "Shall I start at the beginning?" she inquired, taking a sip of her drink.

The beginning was a long way back. Leslie was far from naïve when she married Conrad twenty-five years ago; she was in her late twenties and he was her senior by two decades. She had been through one marriage that lasted scarcely a year, she says, because her husband was mixed up and could only express himself when he had his fist in her mouth. He had been a handsome and aggressive man and in the early days she had equated this aggressiveness with a promise that he would always protect her. The possibility that there was a brutal side never occurred to her. She doesn't resent her first husband, whom she now refers to as "that man"; she just wonders how she could have walked into such a situation. Then Conrad came along after an eighteen-year marriage that had ended in custody cases, courts, and the usual hells. At the time of their meeting he was avoiding any sort of relationship with a woman—even for casual sex—because he was terrified of repeating past mistakes.

Conrad was doing well in publishing and Leslie was moving ahead in an advertising firm. When they were introduced by mutual friends Leslie, who was always attracted to older men, decided she wanted him. It took her a year to win his trust and when they married, she thought of herself as older and wiser and prepared to settle down for life.

Of course, she had considered the inherent problems of marrying a much older man. He might not always be so virile and young but that was something she could accept. Besides, it was years in the future. Every man and woman takes a chance on how long the sexual attraction and performance will last. When their only child, a son, was born she realized that she would likely be a widow and left to finish raising him alone but this was a calculated risk to be faced in the future, and she was sure she would handle it well. Now, all these years later, things are very different from what she envisioned. Leslie stared at me, gave me a small but not sad smile, and recited the facts: Conrad is seventy-two years old, he has had a prostate gland operation and is sexually nonfunctioning; his hips have been operated on and, although he walks, he often shuffles. Sometimes she thinks she married her father. She hastened to reassure me that he is still a proud man who refuses to be useless. His friends visit, he goes to the park, he does the housework. An exceptionally cold assessment? No, not particularly. This is the reality, Leslie pointed out, that some young women being courted by older men should think about. She is contented and loves Conrad still, but she doesn't feel a great many women would feel the same in her circumstances. She is no martyr. She is not beyond satisfying her sexuality else-where, but she considers herself fiercely loyal to her husband. She has learned that loyalty brings its own reward.

Leslie gave me this information very quickly. While I would have openly commiserated with another woman telling me the same story, my increasing awareness of Leslie's sense of dignity ruled this out. I kept thinking so this was Leslie, the lady from New York whom Paul had made seem so mysteri-ous and fascinating. He had briefly described how they had run into each other in a hotel lobby in San Francisco where they were doing some work for their respective companies. Paul is an effortlessly charming and not insincere man who genuinely enjoys striking up conversations. He said something harmless and engaging to Leslie and was impressed immedi-ately with how quick, intelligent, and cheerful she was. He also found that she was an elegant but good drinker, which is something he admires in a woman. I had asked him once how old she was. "Oh, I don't know—of a certain age I suppose. These things don't matter."

Paul travels a great deal on business and after his trips to New York, I heard a few reports of the as-yet-unnamed Leslie who accompanied him to dinner and who rewarded him with her smiles and intellect, not always lovemaking, when he ar-ranged spontaneous champagne breakfasts. To hear Paul tell it, his relationship with Leslie, which took place five years ago and lasted for about a year, was energizing, heavily laden with romance, and crowded with moments of living to the fullest.

There was guilt, of course, because Paul was being un-faithful to his wife, but he will not accept such words as "adul-tery" or "affair" to describe what he once had with Leslie. He needs to feel that most of the wonderful times with Leslie could have been his wife's had she wanted them, though the truth, he told me, was that his wife had pleased him by her sexual aggressiveness in their early years of marriage. Then she gradually lost interest in sex, but not in him. That was very hard for Paul to accept and for years he wondered if she was seeing other men or if he somehow repulsed her. To the best of his knowledge none of this was true; she changed, that's all. First she absorbed herself in their three children, then in a career. It seemed to him that sex was pleasant at times for his wife but not a priority. Paul reasoned that since his wife had such a low interest in sex and since Leslie's husband was incapable of it, they were following a natural path the night they met. Their secret relationship gave them mutual delight and a sense of freedom, and they were not harming anyone.

Paul feels ultimately that his wife is responsible for his unfaithfulness and this is justification in itself. Leslie doesn't feel she has to justify her actions. When sex with her husband was no longer possible, she had no guilt about having brief liaisons when she was traveling. She regarded these hours of pleasure much as she did a deserved meal in a fine restaurant on the company's expense account. Neither she nor Paul intended to leave their spouses. There was too much affection and emotional investment for that. Rather they enjoyed their occasional times together and parted with a lingering sense of affection.

"I have met other people who are in the same boat as I am sexually," Leslie told me. "They stay together for all kinds of reasons. Financial, in particular. But you do care enough not to hurt someone, especially if that person is in ill health. You never abandon anyone for that reason. So I've managed to be discreet and uninvolved. All along the line I realized that if I left my husband I would destroy his world. I might as well give him a gun and watch him shoot himself."

Some couples, she says, don't come to grips with their marital problems until later in life. In the early years they're busy with their children and there's little time for introspection. She thinks the crisis for women of her generation comes after fifteen or twenty years of marriage and it's largely because "women submerge their resentments because they don't want to bring up children alone." Unless a man's sexual behavior is utterly flagrant, many women simply stay in marriage.

But this, however it sounds, is not necessarily the bad bargain it may seem on the surface.

In Leslie's own case, some of the outward characteristics she admired in Conrad in his prime did not last all that long. He was phased out of his company in his early fifties and was never able to recapture the respect or admiration he once took as his due. This eroded him and, to Leslie watching from the sidelines, the progression downward seemed unmercifully swift: from a series of lesser jobs to poor health, to being an old man waiting at home. But his innate worthiness and the thoughtfulness remain. Certainly he is not her lover and only rarely is he a vivacious companion. So she has adjusted her vision. Sometimes, she admits, he seems more like a cherished relative than a husband. Still, he has very legitimate claims on her.

Paul entered her life after she had made a big mistake. A casual affair had developed into love and for a year her emotions swung between intense pleasure and enormous guilt. It reached the point where she had to choose between Conrad and another chance at life. "I spent almost a year trying to make up my mind what was the right thing to do, what I could live with. It kept coming down to this: I accepted an inherent risk when I married an older man. It would be like saying I couldn't stand up to the promise I made. I chose to stay with Conrad and I'm glad I did. I can live with myself and this may be what life is really about."

Conrad has never questioned Leslie about her travels but she would tell him the truth if he asked her. And it would go something like this: Leslie sometimes meets a man she is very attracted to and they go to bed. She can look him in the eye the next morning with no apologies and no regrets, and she goes back home to Conrad because there was and still is devotion, contentment, and a tremendous sense of shared times. Happiness is not a constant, she announces with a little smile.

Her situation requires compromise and she is pleased about how resilient she has become. "There has been a complete reversal of our roles. Conrad was definitely in charge at the beginning and now it is the opposite. I think of him being home and I know he worries if I'm away too long. But he's not morose or sad. He gets lonely but then so do all the wives of all the husbands who travel." Some old, sick people cling but Conrad doesn't. He has his chores and his garden out back of the pleasant home they own within commuting distance of New York City. He reads and visits with the neighbors. And her sexuality, apparently, is her own business.

Leslie says monogamy is wonderful, ideal in fact, if it can be achieved, but it has not been possible for her and in its absence the only thing to do is "try to keep the lying to an absolute minimum." The Leslie of the one-night stands is not a person Conrad need ever know.

After her disastrous love affair, Paul was kind and sympathetic and gave her ego the necessary bandaging. They had a wonderful time together and she is rich in memories of him, but they finally agreed to end their relationship because there was nowhere for it to go. In addition, they were both feeling guilty over the extended deception of their spouses. She didn't want to divide her mind and time anymore. Besides, they both had some repair work to do on their marriages. It was like saying good-bye to someone lovely she had met on vacation. "I sometimes wonder," she said, "what Paul would have done if I had told him I was free, that I had left my husband. I think it would have thrown him into a tailspin."

When I saw Paul again back in Toronto, he was astonished when I told him about Leslie's parting remark. "I can't imagine her saying that," he said, looking distressed. "She knew there was no question of leaving my wife. We came together because we both had unsatisfactory sex lives and she helped me and I think I helped her." Whatever gave her that idea? he wondered again. I tried to tell him that affairs are fraught with tension and excitement and a certain absence of reality, and lovers tend to see them from radically different perspectives.

Although this unexpected remark of Leslie's troubled him briefly, he shrugged it off. After all, Leslie wasn't Paul's *serious* love. She had arrived thirty years after he had met and instantly desired a tall, sophisticated stewardess who was engaged to someone else. He was an inexperienced university graduate who had just started his first job but she married him anyway. It was a time when the only acceptable expression of sexuality was within the framework of marriage, and divorce was a scandal. As Paul explains it: "We went into our marriage with a warmly passionate relationship until after the children were born. I know what you're thinking. 'Where have I heard that before?' But she didn't want any more children and she rejected me fairly quickly. There were months in between lovemaking and I couldn't help feeling there was something wrong with me. I kept saying to myself, 'Here's an attractive, healthy woman and she's not interested.' I did the obvious things: went on a diet, started using mouthwash as the ads tell you. But I still repelled her in some way. It took me a long time to realize that she was just not interested."

For years he went through an almost formalized ritual of persuasion with his wife. He tried patience, then insistence; he courted her anew with flowers and gifts and surprise invitations to cocktails and dinners. He tried gentle conversations to see if he could get at the root of her problem. He bought sex-technique books and, finally, they had a few sessions together with a marriage counselor. Nothing happened. Then the nineteen-sixties arrived with radically changing attitudes to sex and an apparent abundance of available partners. Nothing is as simple as it may appear, but the climate gave Paul every reason to think of himself, to try to restore his sanity. At fifty-two, he is still able to attract the ladies with his perpetually tanned face, his long dark hair, mustache and rakish smile. All in all, he suggests the aging movie matinee idol.

Ten years ago, when Paul decided to seek sex elsewhere, there was something new about him: he suddenly communicated an instant message to some women that he was available, where before he had looked and behaved as the diffident and dutiful husband. Now he seemed confident and able to enter a room and know instinctively which women were not averse to getting acquainted. He didn't just sleep around and he didn't accept every opportunity, but he was pleased indeed to discover that he was not repellent to all women.

There were uncalculated weekends spent with articulate and entertaining women close to his age—surprisingly guilt-free interludes. There were bonuses when he traveled to other cities and could enjoy moments of suspension with nothing to remind him of home. He didn't even bother making the once obligatory telephone call to his wife to assure her his plane hadn't crashed.

If Paul has a philosophy about philandering, it's this: "I can't understand why people who are physically happy with each other get involved physically with someone else. But if you have to satisfy your needs somewhere else, it's not all that bad. It can help to keep marriages together. It has done this for me. There are so many other wonderful things about my marriage—do you realize that I have spent my entire adult life with her? There is too much shared personal history to be disregarded and I consider my responsibilities and my duties to her to be very important. Not many people can find a lover who isn't going to demand everything and that's when you destroy the original marriage."

Keeping his marriage together is essential. His wife is his good friend and there are other things such as loyalty, respect, and habit. Habit, he says, is healthy. But he and his wife seem opposite in life-style. Sexual incompatibility aside, she doesn't share his taste in music and literature and is not deeply interested in the daily comings and goings of his business. Still fashionably thin, she is too voguishly interested in clothes for him. Their serious arguments have been about the raising of their children. He felt he had to be stern because she coddled them too much, and the marriage nearly broke up when two of the children developed alcohol and drug problems.

Leslie was not the most important affair in Paul's life. Months after they ended their relationship, he met another woman at a party who brought him to the brink of divorce and back again to a decision to stay with his wife for good. It developed into a two-year relationship that came close to shattering Paul when it ended. Much younger and single, she was seeing a psychiatrist, but she stopped her therapy once the relationship was established. This was not an ecstatic affair, Paul says, but nice, very friendly. Over the years they became immersed in each other's interests and careers. He remembers the location of every telephone booth he stopped at on his way to work to say good morning. This is the sort of thing he misses most. The physical aspect became less and less important as they found themselves becoming each other's closest friend.

"Almost from the start I told her what we were doing wasn't right. I told her she should have her own man and not someone else's husband. But she said she was against marriage and what we had was fine. I had a place to go, and that had all kinds of wonderful benefits, but I felt guilty. How often can you go to a certain part of town without running into someone you know? I was never able to take her to the theater or to walk with her on the main streets. I couldn't talk about this special person or about what she was accomplishing in her job. Those are horrible things to have missing in a relationship. We discussed my wife in a general way but I never"— Paul paused and gave me a little lopsided smile—"I never said my wife didn't understand me."

His friend continued to have dates because, aside from a lunch or a talk in a park, they only had one night together a week. He kept telling her the relationship would end when she found the right man. And it did. She broke down one night and told him she had found someone she wanted to marry. He kept saying "Marvelous" and meaning it, and at the same time he was thinking, "Oh, Christ!" He left gracefully but he estimates it took him nearly a year to get over her. He tried to resist but he asked her to lunch a couple of times and it was awkward and painful and he quickly said: "I just can't—maybe six months from now we can meet as friends. Maybe you can tell me about your new life." Paul told me there is a lesson here for many men: "I never anticipated such a traumatic thing."

Paul says he has respected his wife through all their years together and considers himself "loyal" to her. He loves and honors her as the mother of his children and for their shared experiences and memories. But he insists that the reason he's still married is that he had a need and fulfilled it somewhere else. He points out that some men love sports almost to the exclusion of their wives and families and this is considered acceptable behavior. But if there's any outside interest in sex, it's considered totally immoral. His upbringing is that if you don't get sex at home, you don't get it anywhere. Even if he had a good physical relationship with his wife, he says he would still require long hours of conversation with different people, including women. That would be moral and he could maintain a position in so-called conventional society. But there's something else few people admit, he says: "Intellectual seduction is more involving than the physical."

He knows his wife must have wondered about him but she never made any accusations. The reason he thought of divorcing her was that he was being torn apart by divided loyalties. He was afraid of hurting her, but on the other hand he reasons that he spared her hurt because if he hadn't found some sexual release he might have walked out on her out of frustration. He believes nothing will break them up now: "She needs me and she takes good care of me. I'd make a lousy bachelor. We have been together too long and we have built up duties and obligations toward each other and I don't want to destroy that."

Paul has had at least one other interlude but no emotional involvement. He is through with that. Yet he believes his affairs saved his marriage and he's not alone in his thinking. I have interviewed marriage counselors and psychiatrists who countenance affairs as a legitimate way to cope with an unsatisfactory marriage in certain circumstances. But it isn't easy to be a divided person and to have to hide so much from the person who is closest to you. Paul can never be sure what his wife knows or that she, who is staunchly traditional, isn't just hanging in there. Because he wavered in his love for her, it is human nature for Paul to wonder on occasion whether his wife has ever thought of leaving him. There is no evidence of it but still there's uncertainty—and it's a price Paul accepts.

I think Paul is a victim of a prevailing sentiment that says a person should be able to satisfy all of another person's needs. It's very hard to accept that we may not be totally fulfilled by a spouse. We all demand this, but staying together often depends on how much we're willing to put up with—or without.

Marlene has looked from both sides now at her twenty-two-year marriage. She endured her husband's affairs and went without an adequate sex life with him even during their reconciliations. Then about ten years ago when her husband, in his infuriatingly sane and sensible manner, confessed under grilling that he thought he was "in love" with his secretary, she decided she was going to look after herself for a change. Her husband, Rod, wasn't pressing for a divorce and she didn't want one either, mostly because her insecurities and fears were stronger than her outrage. Until then she had been as ordinary as apple pie, throwing all her energy into her husband's career, raising their two children and doing volunteer work. Then suddenly, after Rod's confession, she became the kind of woman who seems to belong more to fiction than to fact: the thirty-five-year-old mistress of the seventeen-year-old boy next door.

Marlene had scarcely heard of such a bizarre situation

and certainly there was nothing in her background to prepare her for this kind of middle-life derailment. She and Rod grew up in the same Montreal neighborhood and started going around together at thirteen. They were the traditional child-hood sweethearts who never dated anyone else, and they were virgins when they married after high school graduation. She worked for years as a secretary and in low-management jobs until he received his Ph.D. in mathematics. Any thoughts Marlene might have had of a career were submerged because it was clear to her, and to everyone who knew Rod, that he was brilliant and was going to go far in his future profession as a university professor. They both wanted children very much and she remembers thinking as a bride how lucky those children would be if they had her good looks and his brains. She was proud of the fact that she was earning most of the money and dutifully, if not happily, joined the student wives' association and then the faculty wives'. Whenever there was time, she was a church and hospital volunteer and a political campaigner. It broadened her interests and she loved meeting people, but most importantly, it made her a social asset for her husband, whose rise in the academic world was as swift as she knew it would be.

Outwardly all was domestic bliss. They had two fine babies, an assured place in the community, and a comfortable financial situation. Everything was exactly as they had planned and the only trouble, if that's the word for it, was that their sex life wasn't too exciting. Marlene wasn't sure if she even liked lovemaking all that much. Her husband seemed to want to get sex over with quickly and it would be a long time before she learned anything about prolonged foreplay or French kissing. Nothing seemed to disturb the calm surface until the affair with the secretary. "I was totally taken aback," Marlene said. "I was young and I had kids and I had completely given myself to him. I had leaned on him. Now I was made to feel very inadequate as a woman. He eventually gave up the woman but it made me change terribly."

She assured me this initial affair was very much out of character for Rod but, in retrospect, it probably should not have been all that unexpected. Though not boring, their lives *were* routine, and they had never developed into mature and exciting lovers. She admired Rod's mathematical genius, but so did his secretary, who had a better understanding of his world of lectures, pure research, and scholarly papers. Marlene's interest in mathematics was limited to adding up the grocery list and that sometimes made her feel left out, and a little dumb.

One night, after yet another faculty party when Rod had paid too much attention to his secretary, Marlene reacted in a fit of jealousy and demanded the truth. Rod confessed and said he would go or stay as she pleased. It was a stalemate because she was afraid to let him go and felt heartsick about leaving things the way they were. Rod asked for some time to cool out the romance and then they would try to put their marriage together. Maybe that was reasonable enough for him but Marlene reacted in the classic manner of the wronged woman avenging herself. In rage and despair, she started looking at the men around her and discovered quite a few who were available. Somehow, there was something special about her that made certain men sense she wouldn't reject them. She played around for about a year and was astonished at how eagerly she entered into casual liaisons. She and Rod had resumed the outward appearances of their domestic lives and, armed with a heightened awareness of herself as an attractive woman, it didn't seem to hurt as much to wonder if Rod was still seeing his secretary. They were being proper parents to their children. They were friendly and considerate of each other and their conversations were polite if guarded. Something had been set in motion that was going to take Marlene a lot further than she or her husband could have imagined.

All of a sudden, as she describes it, she became aware of a very strong mutual attraction between herself and Tom, the teenager next-door, who was the children's babysitter and a general pal around the house. Maybe at first it was simply that he flattered her and he looked a little like Burt Reynolds. (She showed me a picture of him to emphasize her point.) She scandalized herself the first time they went to bed in her own house, but it didn't stop her. They remained lovers for nearly six years, all through the time he was reaching young manhood. She admits she's probably the most important factor in the kind of man he has grown to be, and she's a little afraid that this might have been a very wrong thing. She had to force him to have dates with girls his own age for his sake as well as for the sake of appearances. She remembers, with tears, how he despised her when she told him she would not leave her husband and marry him. In order to make him go away, to break the dependency, she told him she had affairs with other men during the summers he was away working. She's not sure he believed her, but it was true.

"Having affairs seemed like a habit I had to feed," Marlene says. "I know I was trying to prove something but I never stopped liking myself. It wasn't sordid and ugly. It was good for me at the time. And my affair with Tom was a beautiful thing for both of us—something I would not have wanted to have missed in my lifetime. I have no regrets for myself but I am sorry that Tom was angry and confused for a long time after we broke up. He moved away, married, and had children and I'm sure he's happy."

She explains that she and Tom were in love; their affair would never have lasted six years if they hadn't been. But obviously it wasn't the meeting of mature minds. There was an emphasis on sexual pleasure—they made love four afternoons a week except when Tom was away for the summers—and it was almost to the exclusion of other forms of communication. Outside the bedroom, she couldn't help but take on a mother role with him, talking to him about his schoolwork, friends, ambitions, and advising him against his wrong notions, one of them being that he would take her away with him. It was a heady experience on a number of levels and she was sure nobody ever became suspicious of Tom since she was so much older. Just your friendly neighborhood mother figure.

For someone who always felt fat and unattractive in front of her husband and who was unsure of herself because he was intellectually superior, Marlene developed quickly into a very self-assured, independent woman—to the extent that she created a part-time job for herself in communications. "But of course," I remarked, "you'd be very good at that." Marlene laughed. Her husband told her many times during the years of the affair and since that she had become much more interesting. She assumes he attributes it to her new work.

Two events seemed to converge that resulted in Marlene and her husband giving up their promiscuous life-style and trying for a real marriage. On one front, Tom was no longer a student and was insistent that she leave her husband and bring her youngest child. But she didn't want to break up her family and she didn't want a divorce. In spite of the messes she and Rod had made, they were compatible and generally liked each other's company. They were both proud of their children and went on outings with them. They continued to care about how the other was feeling and a far more confident Marlene learned to relax a little. Certainly her behavior enabled her to be more forgiving of Rod's actions. When she thought it over, there had been many times when she and Rod had been good to and for each other. In the end, the marriage, even the painful, mixed-up parts, didn't need to be thrown away. "I could see a much happier future but I could not think of just myself and not my family because it had not been all bad with my husband." And there were other reasons why Tom had to go away. The age difference began to seem ridiculous to her and she eventually developed a very bad conscience as she believed more and more that the situation would blow up in her face if she allowed it to continue.

She was willing to try the domestic life again but she had to find out how Rod felt. She knew he had been having an affair with their best friend, whom they had helped through a

nasty divorce. If she would give up Tom and any thought of
future lovers, perhaps he would do the same. They had a con-
frontation, a troubling evening of duo confessions, and finally
decided together that all extramarital sex would end.

Marlene is in her forties now, two years later, and living
a mutually monogamous life with Rod. She seems settled and
pleased with herself. A nonstop conversationalist, she is the
type who will impulsively tell her life story to a stranger at a
party. She knows she is highly emotional and easily given to
intense frustration, but she tries to curb this. We talked for
many hours in her home and she underlined both the humor
and the sorrow of her situation. She recited so many names of
men she had affairs with that I became hopelessly confused—
possibly a dozen men, including one-night stands. At first I
wondered if Marlene might sound like a nymphomaniac in my
writing of her story, but such judgment would miss the point.
Discussing the matter with a male friend, he said: "Have you
looked at it this way: Marlene was doing what some men have
always done and this is to enjoy sex in an uninhibited way. I
think the word nymphomaniac was invented by a malicious,
threatened man. It's too easy to throw that word at women
who admit to the joy of sex."

I think Marlene had an exaggerated need for male approval and part of the blame might be placed on her husband,
who, perhaps unwittingly, didn't do much to enhance her self-
image. Some of Marlene's sexual adventures were acts of sheer
revenge. We all need approval but self-esteem is an inner
development—not the applause of the neighborhood. It had
not been easy to give up her previous life-style but she says it
has brought a measure of peace. She could not be sure that
Rod wouldn't have affairs again but she was sure about herself. "We'll have a really great marriage once the itch is gone,"
she said. "I think that monogamy is the most desirable way of
life even though I know I don't have any right to say it. I'm
getting less frustrated but I would have been frigid by now if
the other things hadn't happened. I don't think I'm very intelli-

gent but I know the warmth that I give to my family. Our kids really like us. I have a lot of friends and an ability to get along with people."

Marlene has changed because of the experiences she's had and she believes she is more of a challenge to her husband. Now she understands and accepts certain childish things about him that he can't help. She is facing the future with a sense of commitment and it's a commitment she genuinely wants. The sexual ecstasy is over and she's honest enough to say she misses it. "You have to wind down. I feel contented but that's because I'm busy and I'm not just a housewife. I've replaced my sexual frustrations with my business. I think you have to replace things in your life."

Leslie, Paul, and Marlene came to the brink of replacing their spouses but they didn't. They are rather extreme examples of couples who are staying together despite serious outside relationships. Each in his or her own way needed the permanence of marriage.

Perhaps there was more folly than wisdom along the way but some sort of victory might be implied. Clearly it doesn't seem a happy or noble victory, and some people may find them less than admirable types. But one thing can be said about them: They know, more than many people, whom they can live with—and without.

4

Inevitable Dalliance
Affairs

When I met Rita the first time I was struck by how dark and very attractive she was, a description she would say didn't fit her a few years ago. She looks people right in the eye and her welcome is there for all to see. One sees in her eyes a resolve that she is going to be utterly frank about herself. Before I have merely taken her hand, I cannot shake the initial feeling that she has rehearsed herself and I am here for the purpose of catharsis; an impression which turns out to be true.

My meeting with Rita arose from a discussion with her husband, Martin, during a business meeting. When I told him I was going to write a book about lasting relationships he said eagerly: "My wife and I have a wonderful marriage. Our twentieth wedding anniversary is coming up. Why don't you interview us?" I stepped back and wondered how perfect any marriage could be.

I was thinking of Martin's unbridled enthusiasm for his wife and his marriage as I walked to their home to meet Rita. They live in a central area of Toronto where the houses are old and brick and somewhat out of the range of the average person's bank account. The huge trees form a cathedral-like arch over the sidewalks. Rita, standing in the doorway, looked fragile and there was a warning intensity about her large, dark eyes. As she showed me through her rooms (I admired her for showing me the house), she surprised me by suddenly turning toward me and saying with an ironic smile, "I created my dream house during the ugliest period of my life. Martin was having an affair with a typist in his office at the time." I didn't know what to say but Rita was not at a loss for words. "When I found out about the affair I said things I could not believe were coming out of my own mouth. But he did things that I have never forgotten."

Looking around Rita's house I saw no hint of early years of struggle with Martin, but this was not what her childhood house had been. I soon learned that she was raised by a father who was a drunkard and a womanizer, and a mother who put up with it. There were bill collectors at the door and Rita was always scared growing up, never knowing what she would find when she came home after school. She says her greatest need has always been security, a need which led her to believe as an adolescent that there would someday be a real man to look after her. When she quit school at sixteen at the top of her class, no one suggested that she could have a career instead of a job. Now there is residual bitterness about this. When Rita looks at the opportunities for women today she remembers the old code of conduct about getting married and being cared for that narrowed her life.

A certain determination accompanied that code: if she couldn't get away from it she would be better at following it than anyone else she knew. She has taken strict care of herself and does not look like a woman old enough to have a daughter of marriageable age and a son in senior high school. The fact that she is very close to her children is apparent in the respect that they show her. She has had no serious problems with them. There was some sibling rivalry—she uses psychiatric catchwords easily because she is intensely interested in reading about the development of the human personality—but her children were never at each other's throats. It was her role to see to that; to see to everything.

If the children had any brushes with drugs or alcohol or adolescent sexual disasters, they must have been minor because Rita never found out. Instead she talked about their many childhood illnesses, which she took very hard. She told me of their achievements and ambitions and I sensed that they have turned out well because although she kept them on a short rein, she was always there when they needed her. Following the code of her own childhood, Rita tried to be the perfect wife and mother. And she very nearly was.

It wasn't easy living up to the high standards she set for herself but it was worth it. Her husband was becoming more successful as a lawyer every year. He was home every night and his affection and pampering more than compensated for the miserable memories of her drunken, betraying father. Life had definitely seemed on the upswing for fifteen years when suddenly Martin announced that he was having an affair. Rita stunned me with her frankness about what happened.

"I hated him for making such a fool of me," she told me. "I hated him when I remembered the time he took me and that girl to lunch and smiled at both of us and I didn't know that she was his little whore."

As she calmly poured tea into tiny cups, Rita said she was not the same woman anymore. "I'm probably a better one. You don't go through that kind of experience and emerge on the same level. I no longer function as a superwoman and I don't think of Martin as flawless, although I think he's probably better than most men." Perhaps, she suggested, if we went over the first fifteen years of their marriage in detail some sense of what went wrong might emerge.

After dropping out of school Rita worked for a few years in secretarial jobs almost dreaming her days away until she met the right man. She was nineteen when she married Martin and, more than love, she remembers how grateful she was that he was strong and could remove her from an intolerable situation. They wanted children and had them quickly. There wasn't much money and Rita was almost schoolgirlishly happy, describing their evenings out as young married people, going to a movie or taking a walk and having a sandwich in a restaurant.

Life seemed so normal and untroubled until Rita noticed that Martin had developed an oddly distant attitude toward their two children. Martin's own father had been a stern and unaffectionate man, and the lesson he took from his childhood was that it is necessary for a man to earn a good living. This became his measure of true success and Rita came to realize that Martin's obsession with his image would mean she was going to have to raise these children alone. "When they were infants he would get up in the night with them and he loved feeding them. But as soon as they became little people he found it difficult to relate to them. He didn't give them any creative time. He was happy to let me take over. He had complete confidence in my ability with the home and the children. The conflict for me was that my children wanted me totally and so did Martin." Sometimes she would plead with him to be more involved with the children's activities but he was so awkward and unnatural that she let it slip by and finally accepted her role as supermom. She meted out the discipline, saw that her children were beautifully dressed and well mannered, and made his house shine. It bothered her, but she reasoned that there were worse problems in the world, and she and Martin loved each other dearly. She had her idealized marriage, the approval of her family and friends, and no portents of troubled times. Rita says: "As far as everybody, including me, was concerned, it was Rita and Martin *forever.*"

Martin's legal career was flourishing, and just when everything seemed to be going well, something started to go very wrong. His personal measurement for success—his ability to make a good living—seemingly betrayed him. His work wasn't really satisfying after all and he became brooding and introspective. At this point in the story, Rita paused to make the type of sweeping statement that she has earned the right to make: she said the need for sheer survival holds many families together because they don't have the time to sit around and wonder what's wrong. "It's a *fact*," she told me. "You can examine your life to death."

Then there were other events, sad in themselves, that Martin seemed to pack together into a huge ball of depression. His parents died within a short period of time. Then an older brother he loved also died. Suddenly he didn't want to go to the office, but once there, he felt little urgency to come home since Rita, as usual, was taking care of everything on that front. All he told her was that he was miserable for reasons he couldn't understand. Rita doesn't know at what point in this jumble the typist entered the picture but she said, with ill-concealed disgust, that it was a "classic case." Martin was miserable and so was his typist, who confided to him that her husband was neglecting her. It began with sympathetic lunches.

On discovering adultery, wives need to find someone or something to blame other than themselves—the midlife crisis, a younger woman looking for a father figure, an ambitious, scheming woman attracted to a man for his money and power, or the eternal vamp who thrives on conquest. It's too hurtful to consider that your husband is in love with someone else. Some men, who clearly aren't in love with their lovers, also accept cliché explanations for their behavior, but others are very uncomplicated in their attitude toward adultery. I remember a man in his forties, very successful, subject to fits of ennui but blessed with a fairly rewarding marriage, who told me that a young, ambitious woman joined his staff, blatantly invited him to lunches, and announced over the pâté: "I'm going to get you." And she did, for a while. His marriage nearly broke up and I asked him why he took the chance. "Would you believe me if I told you that I simply *wanted* to have an affair?"

Rita and I traded stories about the classic reasons for adultery. We agreed that there are many elements at work in affairs and decided that the clandestine in itself might be just as exciting as the other man or woman. "But that's no comfort when it's happening to you," Rita pointed out. "First you spend a lot of time trying to pinpoint something that should have warned you. Later, after the shock wears off, you wonder about the things you might have done wrong." I told her what an acquaintance of mine once said to me of her feelings after her husband's infidelity. She decided to experience these novel emotions and not to look for any answers. "You're just like a widow," she said. "You go through the sense of loss and the numbness of feeling and the anger. But there's no coffin and no body and therefore no reasonable expectation of a burial."

Five years later, Rita says all she can do is accept Martin's interpretation of the situation, which she continues to examine in detail. Martin told her then and still maintains that he was going through a midlife crisis and is convinced that he was "insane" at the time.

In the early days before Rita knew of the affair, she would not allow herself to think of the possibility that there was another woman. Certainly Martin was depressed and withdrawn, but he still called her twice a day from the office, even if he didn't say anything, and he came home every night, even though he might as well not have been there. During those months they sold their house and she began decorating their new one. Rita, still enraged at the memory, said Martin didn't lift a finger to help. "I had to pick out every goddamn brick and doorknob. This was supposed to be my dream house; I was dying to move here and I should have been so excited. But I had the heaviest heart. I didn't know why."

In keeping with the classic "adultery" formula, it now seems that just about everybody else knew. People in the office, some of her relatives, and many of their friends were busy gossiping about "poor Rita." Crying one night, she called her sister and asked what she could do about Martin. "When she said, 'He might have a girlfriend,' I hung up the phone but I just knew it was true. The next day I called Martin at work and asked him to meet me for a coffee. He told me to leave him alone, that he'd be all right."

But he came and Rita remembers how horrible he looked and how awful she felt. Women who are placed in this cold, ultimately cringing position of confronting their husbands are seldom original in their approach, but Rita's wording was different, to say the least. "I said to him, 'Is it possible you have had an indiscretion and that you're feeling so guilty you can't function?' He said, 'It isn't an indiscretion. I'm in love with another woman.' At that moment I died. That was the end to me."

On the way home she drove the car like a zombie saying to herself, "Oh we're so close he even wants to share the fact that he loves this woman. He just wants to go away with her somewhere. He's glad I know, he can't stand the guilt. He doesn't even know if he wants a divorce, but we must all be discreet because she's married. *Well, so am I!*"

When she got home, Rita made lunch for her children, she knows that, and then she called a friend who had gone through the same thing. Martin went back to his office, informed his girlfriend that his wife knew about their affair, and then he came home early looking very unlike a man who was in love. They told their children they were upset and needed to be alone and went into the den. They talked for hours, and Rita recalls: "I was hating him and shivering. It was the longest night of my life."

Martin told her he thought he was going to have a nervous breakdown. Unbelievably, the girlfriend kept calling on the telephone while they talked, which made Rita hysterical. Now she still can't believe how she and Martin talked and acted that night. "I said, 'Take a knife and kill me. You're killing me anyway.' That was the only time I made a threatening gesture. I never planned suicide. He finally made an arrangement to meet the girl at nine-thirty and I went upstairs. He followed me and put his arms around me. I said, 'Get away, you *smell* like her.'"

He told her he had no place to go and she replied evenly that there were such things as hotels and relatives. Then, with no explanation or warning, he simply said he was staying with her. Rita still doesn't understand that moment. It wasn't love because she knows he hated her for a while. It could have been the sheer exhaustion of a sick and guilty man. It may have been no more than timing. In his condition if he had been with his girlfriend he might have stayed with her. But he was here in his wife's bedroom and the fight had gone out of him. It was a raw moment of needing sleep and peace at any price. Perhaps there was the perception that there never was any clear-cut choice. He would be wounding people no matter what he did.

There is little more to that particular evening that Rita is compelled to talk about. Martin eventually went to his girlfriend's house, told her it was over and returned home with red eyes. He put his head on her shoulder and cried and told her it was the hardest thing he had done in his life. "And that's another thing I hated him for," Rita said. "He said this to me when we had two kids and miscarriages, when we had held babies with croup in the shower. And these few months with a little whore was the hardest thing he had to give up."

She went to a psychiatrist the next day and then both she and Martin became involved with a therapeutic community for several months. She admitted the community was somewhat messianic and had a reputation for being outside the mainstream of traditional therapy, but she says they were helped. In effect, she was told that her husband had been wonderful up to a point and was almost too good to be true. But in spite of all kinds of advice, the next nine months were like a living lie and they affected her physically. She couldn't eat and although she became more attractive as she lost weight, it didn't matter to her, nor, she was sure, did it matter to anyone else. "My children gave me a lift but nothing I did gave me any pleasure. I found myself running out of supermarkets because I was afraid I would start screaming. The gossips were telling me Martin was there only because of the children, and Martin was trying to convince me that he had never planned to leave me." She's not so sure about that even though he never stopped cuddling her in bed, and eventually she began to initiate lovemaking. With therapy, Martin eventually became more himself but with a difference. "He was able to talk about his feelings and he became an emotional person. He wasn't just the stern father and the good provider anymore. He actually laughed and cried and got angry." Rita suddenly looks exasperated. "Why couldn't he have just had a roll in the hay? It would have been so much easier. But no, he had to be in *love!*"

Rita remembers that the main thing that came out of therapy was that she and Martin were too wrapped up in each other and had hopelessly idealistic expectations. They had to stop pretending they could provide all of each other's needs. A practical suggestion was that they develop different interests that didn't include the other partner. Martin now plays golf a few days a week and Rita is taking university courses. "I'm so pleased," she told me. "It's nice to know that your brain hasn't atrophied over the years. I also like to travel and play tennis and go out with my friends. I deserve it. Now Martin and I enjoy the time we spend together more than we ever did."

Although Rita still thinks of Martin's affair five years after it happened, she tries to be realistic about it. She rationalizes that there was only one bad year out of twenty years of marriage and it gave them the impetus to work out their problems. "Can you understand when I say that I'm glad it happened?"

I told her I had heard many women say the same thing. I remember one such woman I met at a party in Philadelphia who described the dramatic change in her personality after she discovered her husband's three-year love affair. They were living in an American business colony in Europe and she threw herself into the party life from which her husband was somewhat excluded because he couldn't speak the native language. She loved attention from men and she indulged in the most bizarre activities; she even waded through public fountains at dawn. She thought her husband was sweet to indulge her, but what he was really doing was escaping into the company of a quiet, intelligent woman who gave him all of her attention.

"His affair forced me to confront the ludicrous spectacle of myself. I finally grew up. I'm now an expert in medieval art and I am respected for it. Most of all I respect myself. Strange as it sounds, I'm very grateful to my husband for forcing me to see what I was."

Rita says the good that has come out of her experience is that she still loves Martin but in a mature way, not as some knight who rescued her. We discuss how hard it is to totally forget the past and she says she is a little sorry she spent so much time talking about the affair. She reassures me. "When I am happy," Rita says with a smile, "I am the happiest I have ever been."

It was awkward a few weeks later when Martin and I shook hands in his office, which Rita had decorated much in the chrome-and-acrylic style of their home. He seemed to sink back in a chair far removed from me, looking as if he expected some sort of criticism. He is a small, youthful man who dresses very conservatively one day and then wears something outrageous from the latest boutique the next. He has a very pleasing manner and there's no doubt he's attractive to women. I feel his initial embarrassment and I admire him for going through with the interview. Knowing Rita's emotionalism and her honesty, I'm sure he must have wondered if we had ganged up on him.

Martin told me his first impression of married life was that he would be the head of the household and that his wife, like his mother, would look after the children. He described how some unexpected feelings crept in when his children were born. "I had this lonely, empty feeling the night my daughter was born. I didn't realize how much I depended on my wife's attention and now I had some competition. Rita took on the responsibility and I can't recall us arguing that I didn't spend enough time with my daughter, but I guess Rita sees it that way. It was always easy to drop the kid off on the in-laws. I envy the relationship of other fathers with their kids, their warmth and respect. Our kids went to Rita first and I was envious of that too, but that's the way it was. It's as if she had three children in the house."

When he married Rita, she gave him a great deal of confidence because she was so intelligent. She was a compliment to him but he was slightly troubled that she wasn't looking toward a career. Back in 1963, before women's lib, he was telling her that she should be more than an aspiring lawyer's wife. "I wasn't trying to put her down, but she just wasn't interested. We were so happy that even on fifty dollars a week we felt lucky." He remembers one time she asserted herself and insisted she would take over handling the family finances. He laughs and says she was so hopeless that he started keeping all pressures from her. He acknowledges that he treated her like a princess.

From their different ideas about children and Rita's sheltered existence, Martin's monologue moved swiftly to the heart of the *affair*. Unlike Rita, he does not have a before-the-affair and after-the-affair view of his marriage. He looks at the whole picture as being good, especially the past few years. "I feel I went through the 'male menopause' at the age of thirty-seven. This is when a man begins to wonder about his life, when he starts to blame everything on circumstances. After my mother died, I had an affair and I lost my perspective, my sense of values. I was going to leave my wife and my family and go and live with this woman. I tried to rationalize it and say I was going for the younger woman who was prettier, but they were both intelligent and pretty. I would sit down and ask why I was doing this. It made no sense but I was caught up in it. I guess it was the excitement. I think the pleasure was only in the sneaking and in the conquest. But I wasn't capable of handling it. It had to have an end."

Martin is a moral man and he tried to justify himself by saying he was in love, but, more often than not, he thought he was out of his mind. He received tremendous positive support from his lover, but he got this from his wife too. Maybe it was because Rita's support had become predictable.

From the beginning, the other woman made it clear that she was very available and suddenly Martin was in love over his head. He would sit home nearly crying but he could never tell Rita why. One night he turned to her and demanded: "Do you expect me to love you and have the same feelings as we had when we were first married?" She said, "Yes or we can't stay married."

The day Martin admitted his affair to Rita has the same nightmarish quality for him as it had for her. As he recalls it, things moved very swiftly. "I came home and I didn't know what I was doing. But I had to see how Rita was. She was crying. I put my arms around her and said, 'Do you want to know how it happened?' She said she didn't want to know anything. The next thing I knew I was telling my girlfriend that I couldn't leave my wife." Inside he was a whirlwind of conflicting thoughts and emotions. On the one hand, he felt he should stay with Rita because of the children. He had always been such a "good boy." He rarely drank. He hadn't had sex before he was married. He had never had an affair before. On the other hand, he was over thirty, life was passing him by, and he'd better catch up on what he'd missed.

Martin doesn't fantasize anymore. He doesn't want a friendship with any other woman because it's just too complicated. But he firmly believes that if a man is alive he will always be tempted. The only time he thinks of the affair is when he sees other people going through the same thing. "There is no longing anymore, absolutely not. It was a growing-up experience and my life is much better now." Rita had said that when they were first going through therapy she felt Martin hated her. He told me he was very cold at the time because he felt he had more than paid his dues. Rita was punishing him too much. "She wasn't about to forgive easily. It was all over and we were in therapy and I still had to grovel. So naturally there was anger against her, but at the same time I wanted to help her get through it."

In therapy they were told that loving is letting go and they accept this. Even though they know that they need each other very much, they've learned that too much dependency can be suffocating, and because each is now stronger individually, their marriage is that much more secure.

Victoria and Alex are not married but they have been living together for eight years and expect to keep it that way for the rest of their lives. She loves him even more since her affair of a year ago because he did none of the things a man might be expected to do in those circumstances. Every counselor or psychiatrist I interviewed told me that, as difficult as infidelity is for a woman, most men are devastated and go into complete shock. Always the benefactor of the double sexual standard, a man, generally speaking, is culturally and emotionally unprepared for the unfaithfulness of his partner, while women are raised with the thought that they may have to face infidelity someday.

What Alex didn't do was walk out on Victoria. He did not seek revenge through other women. He did not constantly bring up the affair and he has never used it in their arguments. When Victoria drove away for a few days to clear her head, Alex did something that was unusual for anyone, and almost heroic for him. He went to a psychiatrist.

An aloof man, Alex opened up usually only to long-established friends, and he always considered himself intelligent enough to handle anything that came his way. Before Victoria's affair, he wouldn't have believed that *he* was going to spill out his pain to some professional problem-solver. But when the time came he responded to a sad curiosity that demanded to know what there was about him or his relationship with Victoria that would make her behave so un-

characteristically. He had to admit to himself that he couldn't
find the answer alone.

Victoria didn't need a professional opinion about her behavior. The affair was a desperate act and she was willing to
chance the consequences. "Alex needed a sharp and ugly lesson to shake him out of his complacency," she told me. "And I
needed to know that being sexually desirable was not all that
great or what I wanted at all."

When Alex and Victoria met, both were in the process of
getting divorces after about a decade of marriage with partners who seemed a good choice at the beginning, before they
began to dissolve with a lot of pain and spitefulness. They
moved in together and were happy for seven years in a civiliz-
ing, loving, and carefully nurtured relationship, before Victoria began to sense unmistakable signs that this "marriage"
was also withering away. So she made her moves toward an
affair.

There were several vulnerabilities converging when Victoria became unfaithful. She is very overweight and constant
dieting has not resulted in any lasting improvement. Her self-
image is as erratic as the numbers she reads on her bathroom
scales, and at forty-two she is nearly five years older than
Alex, who is unusually youthful-looking. Added to this is a
rather "maternal" aspect of love that Victoria sometimes re-
veals.

Age difference didn't bother Victoria constantly because
she has extraordinary skills as a hostess and an ability to make
close friends and attract interesting acquaintances. Alex's social reticence was always compensated for by the fact that he
could be very open and revealing in Victoria's company alone.
For years they were able to talk about everything, their feelings, their love, and their problems. Then a year ago a domestic pall settled over the household. There was no discernible
dissatisfaction but, rather, an air of tired familiarity. Conversations were suddenly limited to three unromantic topics: Victoria's teenaged daughter, who lives with them, the renova-

tions on the house, and the success of Alex's advertising agency. Victoria, who demands openness and returns it fully, was miserable, frustrated, and scared. If she let the situation continue, there would soon be no relationship left.

"I deliberately had an affair," Victoria confided to me before Alex joined us. "I needed to know I was still desirable because Alex was ignoring me sexually as well. I was absolutely desperate and I was prepared to do anything to change this half-dead life we were living. One night when we were having a party I got drunk and made sure Alex caught me and the man in a very compromising situation. It was a shameful thing to do but I wanted to shock him back to his senses. He could either leave me or face the fact we had problems and we *both* had to work them out."

And just possibly, Victoria admits, there was an element of wanting to meet her fears dead on. She always worried that Alex might be seeing another woman; after all, her former husband had put her through that humiliation and Alex had been unfaithful to his wife with Victoria. These feelings also seemed to make sense because Alex's cold behavior was some sort of betrayal. This impasse was making her feel as chilled as when her marriage had suddenly collapsed. More and more she seemed to be looking back at that ruin of a marriage.

Victoria met her husband, an American, in England, where she was born. He brought her to Philadelphia and they settled down into an amicable, if unremarkable, marriage. He was becoming a successful banker and they had their little daughter, Cheri, who was precious to both of them. But the previously slim Victoria never lost the extra weight after the baby's birth and she started gaining more. She insists the marriage was fine for eight out of the eleven years. The only problem she zeroes in on is her weight. "My being fat seemed to bother him more and more and, at the same time, he hated my diets and exercises. He despised it when we went to a restaurant and I started counting calories." But she learned to live with this. After all, she had a responsible job with a school board, which she enjoyed, and they had a "lovely coterie of friends." Without any warning, as Victoria explains it, everything blew up in her face. Her husband, who was approaching forty, seemed to become obsessed with the question of what he was really accomplishing in his life. Before she knew it, he reacted by abruptly leaving her for his twenty-one-year-old secretary.

"Why didn't he do something *original?*" she moans, and then says she thinks she knows why he went off the track. "He was so serious and ambitious that he never had any time to play around as a young man. When he ran off from me, the first thing he did was get this neat car and grow his hair long."

He walked out on her in the summer just before they were to go to their seashore place, but she and her daughter Cheri went by themselves anyway. "I think it was about ten minutes after we drove off that he came back and installed his girlfriend in our house," she says. "I hated him for that. It showed a very disgusting side of his nature." There was no thought on her part of any attempt at reconciliation.

Alex, who had been listening to Victoria with me, touched briefly on the salient points of his ten-year marriage. The first few years seemed fine. He had made it clear to his wife that he wanted no children; he didn't like them and wasn't going to pretend otherwise. This was a bitter disappointment for his wife, and to make up for it she kept a menagerie of fifteen cats. Bored and disgusted, he started frequenting the better bars with a succession of women. Victoria, who was looking for any balm for her shattered ego, had plunged into the same singles scene with a vengeance, and it was inevitable that the two would meet. They were attracted from the beginning and within three months Alex moved in with Victoria and Cheri.

Victoria was very flattered by the attention of a young, attractive man, but she did not expect the romance to last. Victoria's attitude suggested that she was afraid that a bad marriage tends to repeat itself. Alex, on the other hand, was prepared for more of a commitment and wanted to marry her right from the beginning. A man of orderly mind and correct demeanor, he wanted the legitimacy of marriage to end any speculation that they were merely "shacking up."

Victoria has never allowed Alex to discipline her daughter, who was nine when he began living with them. Cheri thinks of him as her friend and not as a parental figure. Victoria asks his advice about Cheri and sometimes they make joint decisions, such as the recent one not to buy her a car because her school marks were so poor. Always the perfectionist, Alex felt that she deliberately chose not to do well. He was also appalled when Cheri developed a typical adolescent romance with the telephone. It infuriated him to come home and see her giggling and gabbing for hours. Victoria understands this strictness in him because he was raised by a mean-spirited father who made it clear he detested children and sent Alex away to live permanently with relatives at the age of thirteen. Still, it has been a fairly smooth trip with the child and Alex enjoys describing himself as a family man.

Alex would never have discussed Victoria's affair with me if she had not turned to me during the interview and said: "You're sitting next to a totally monogamous male. He expects monogamy and it's also very important to me." She paused: "But I was unfaithful to him." I looked at Alex and saw his jaw tighten and asked if it would bother him to talk about it.

"It was a brutal experience," he said tersely. "I suppose it taught me something." Victoria reminded him that before the affair they had gradually stopped talking about anything real. He wouldn't express his intimate feelings; she couldn't even draw him into a fight to clear the air. "I was a quiet, private person who wanted to keep everything to myself," Alex explains, "but Victoria wouldn't stand for it." He understood her need for constant examination about how their lives were proceeding, but the conversations attempted to draw some kind of performance out of him that he didn't possess. He was better suited to being quiet with her in the same room. Too many words and emotions made him uncomfortable.

Alex could better accommodate himself to the action-and-success attitude of his advertising agency and he found himself completely preoccupied with business. Victoria says: "If something bothers me I speak right out. I would get a sharp retort and he would walk away. I couldn't stand the distance he was creating." The affair certainly brought about the reevaluation of their relationship that Victoria so desperately wanted but the aftereffect was that they spent three angry months under the same roof without a semblance of the closeness they had once felt.

"My first reaction to the affair," Alex says, "was 'goodbye, lady.' Then I remembered this doctor who was sort of a friend of mine and I kept telling myself that he'd probably heard this story a thousand times. It wouldn't be as if I was shocking him or revealing anything new. I knew I had to straighten myself out some way. He was able to steer my thinking in the right directions, he was helpful but I sorted it out by myself. I recover quickly in stress situations. What I needed was to recover my male ego." He knew he had to learn to come out of himself if he was going to continue living with Victoria's demand for open communication. They both say now that if their new openness leads to a little verbal fistfighting, so much the better.

Alex had two random thoughts he wanted to contribute before I left and he spoke very seriously. Men should recognize there is such a thing as a male menopause, a time of complete disorientation. "It happens to a lot of men as they get older and they should prepare for it. They should not make the mistake of thinking they're the only ones going through it. They should read about it, talk to other men, talk to their doctors, even discuss it with their wives if they can. It might help them consider before they make a possibly wrong decision." And further, consideration of each other every moment of the day almost guarantees a lasting marriage or relationship, Alex believes.

As Victoria was driving me to the place where I was staying, she mentioned that I hadn't asked them about their sex life, which had been nonexistent at one point. Well, how is it? I asked her. "It's not as frequent as when we were first together," she said, "but it is still very good. Sex fell apart early on with my husband. The difference is that Alex genuinely doesn't mind that I'm fat."

I told Victoria I hoped there wasn't going to be any scene when she returned home, that I felt a little nervous when they were *communicating*—actually they worked up quite an argument about whether Alex thought she would ever have another affair, and he admitted he found that impossible to believe. She laughed and said it was fine, it was good for them. "I'm quite surprised," she told me. "I knew Alex would go along with the interview because I sort of insisted, but I didn't think he would reveal himself. I like that. I think it augurs very well for us. Don't you?"

5

Once More With Feeling
Second Marriages

Elizabeth, who is forty-four years old, still believes marriage should be permanent even after an unfortunate choice of a first husband. She doesn't have the excuse that she was too young when she married, but she knows now that she was naïve. She knew her husband as a bon vivant during their two-year engagement but she expected him to change after marriage and take on the responsibilities of a husband, something he never did. She ignored all the proofs that they were mismatched because she was determined that her marriage would somehow be perfect. Raised with this expectation, Elizabeth had as an example the thirty-year marriage of her parents, which, in her remembering of it, had never been marred by arguments or unkind words. After she became a widow, Elizabeth's mother told her she could scarcely remember a day when she did exactly as she pleased. Elizabeth's father had created their lives and she was incapable of questioning his authority. But the knowledge that her mother was not entirely happy, whether it would have mattered or not, came long after Elizabeth was married. "I made all the classic mistakes," she told me. "I was romantically deluded. I demanded he be what he wasn't and I gave up all my personal goals in order to be his loving wife and a marvelous hostess for his fascinating friends. I turned him off completely and I finally left when I became too sick and lonely."

Elizabeth kept a very low profile when she left her husband and her control over pain was admirable. Her marriage had consisted of highs and lows with nothing in between, and she deliberately sought the company of quiet, dependable men. Instead of the glamorous parties she was used to, she opted every time for a movie or dinner for two. In some respects, she had to admit that her life was sometimes dull. "But I had been through hell with an exciting and brilliant person and the next man in my life was going to be his complete opposite." During this period when she was feeling low-spirited, she met Anthony. They dated for six months with neither of them expecting much to come of it. Anthony was frank about the fact that he had never stayed long with one woman. When they took an apartment together, it was with the understanding that they would probably part, and they promised each other that they would behave in a civilized manner. There was a certain sense of wonderment on her part when Elizabeth and Anthony got married two years later. She also admits to being ruthlessly practical about their relationship. Even though her basic nature is against living together, she insisted that it was the only way to be sure about another man.

"It really worked for us. We knew everything about each other and had discussed every possible topic. No children because I was older and also because we both recognized that he would have to come first with me. I knew it was important to him to be the head of the household and this didn't bother me in the least. I was established in a career and he admired me for this and he liked most of my friends. Anthony's one reservation was that our relationship and our love life might change. The only thing that happened was that he relaxed more."

Her second marriage of six years is working beautifully and Elizabeth strongly believes this would not be so if it hadn't been for the terrible times she went through with her first husband. She describes herself as being more patient and devoid of any desire to change her husband's ways. Although she has been a loud supporter of women's liberation, out of her own experience, total equality in marriage is a myth. "If you're opting for this you're better off to live on your own and have lovers. Most men still want to feel that they're running the household. I know that I pamper him outrageously, but then so does he. The wonderful thing is that neither of us keeps track."

I have kept a personal record on Elizabeth over our many years of friendship and I know how solid her second marriage is, and how determined she is not to disillusion herself or repeat her mistakes. Because of her and the other remarried couples I came to know, there is perhaps one statement that can be made about them that would not necessarily apply to people married for the first time: A measure of their hope for the future is bound up in vastly improving on the past.

I had a little advance information about Vincent and Carrie before we met. A former professor of theirs told me they were working on advanced degrees in philology and he considered them both to be on the border of genius or beyond. He said if they ever became more aggressive about money and personal recognition, they would be capable of making original contributions to their field. He also told me Vincent belonged to a family that is both well known and revered around the world; if I let on I knew this we probably wouldn't have an interview. It was interesting that in a city like Los Angeles, where everyone seeking success trades on his connections, Vincent and Carrie were almost recluses.

Because of their admiration for their professor, the couple agreed to see me but seemed to be throwing obstacles in my path about our place of meeting. They suggested hotels and coffee shops, all inappropriate for a personal conversation. I kept asking about their house but they insisted I would never be able to find it. Finally, they relented. It was above a narrow street, almost an alley, on one of the hills out-side central Los Angeles and as I looked up, I knew there was a dwelling somewhere although obscured by the trees and bushes. "We're here," Carrie called as I walked up cracked stone stairs to a little house that was falling apart. Inside were rags and ends and broken springs. The refreshments offered were instant coffee or a glass of water. It was quite a contrast to the white wine or Perrier given me by women in expensive tennis outfits and the martinis from some hard-driving career couples. I could see they were embarrassed—they needn't have been—because they live in a city where people are judged by obvious symbols of success.

My immediate perception of them as a couple was their gentleness and mutual consideration, their maturity and their patience and hope for a future in spite of their precarious financial situation. They sometimes wonder how realistic they are as they continue advanced studies at a time when in California and elsewhere the chances of obtaining a position in their specialty are slight. Vincent has worked part time as a bus driver and Carrie is a check-out girl in a grocery store, and they just manage to keep themselves and Carrie's son from her first marriage together. They have never accepted help from anyone. This is not obstinate pride but a determination that someday they will find the correct pattern for their lives and it will work for them.

Vincent is tall, lean, and blond, a pleasant-looking man who seems younger than thirty-five. There is nothing striking about him; he is relaxing, but there seems very much a pur-pose to what he does, a quest for answers even in an in-significant moment. For example, he recalls looking at a par-ticularly beautiful flower and describing it to Carrie and realizing, with pleasure, that she was seeing this flower with his same eyes.

Carrie is thirty-two and has a well-kept body. She's in-teresting to look at, with her thick, curly hair and outsized glasses. Vincent was first attracted to her because of her seriousness and her intelligence. They had known each other casually on campus and they were both at a crossroads when they came together five years ago. Their marriages had failed and both were living with people who were clearly as wrong for them as their former spouses.

Vincent doesn't speak vindictively of his first wife, but she was bored and boring. Their marriage was comfortable and friendly but they had nothing in common. Eventually they both admitted that they had made a mistake. There was little intimacy and they didn't have the same vision of life; Vincent says he felt lonely with her. They met in high school and she was his first girl. When he went into the Navy, he felt alone and scared and asked her to marry him. They stayed together in growing disillusionment for six years. He describes his marriage as a fantasy with no roots in reality. "I think my wife knew we were going to break up. The person who's going to leave doesn't feel as badly about it as the person who's going to be left. I became aware of other possibilities for my life and I saw our relationship as a limitation. When people talk of their marriages failing, I think in a lot of cases the marriages were okay as far as they went. They may have been rewarding but it just wasn't enough."

Although he is convinced of the correctness of his decision to leave his first wife, Vincent is a humane man who still feels sorrow that he had to go through a marriage and then hurt another person in order to finally find the kind of love and serenity he has now. He feels that this kind of looking backward doesn't accomplish anything, but he's honest enough to face it. He doesn't try to justify himself but attempts to maintain a certain perspective on his past. "Your potential in life depends on the receptivity of your partner. If you are expressing yourself to a vacuum, you might as well be alone. It may be selfish because the other person suffers too." He doesn't condemn anyone for drifting from one relationship to another, but he believes you are a limited person if you won't accept commitment and intimacy.

Carrie has the same wistfulness as Vincent when she speaks of her first marriage, a mistake she made at an early age. At eighteen she married an older man with a different cultural background who locked her into a domestic situation, treated her like a child, and even refused to allow her to learn to drive a car because it would take her outside the confines of her home, where she belonged. When their son, Todd, was born, the rules became more rigid. Carrie's outlook began changing and as she developed strength her husband tried harder to keep her under his domination. After seven years of marriage, she walked out on him and her son because she knew what she was missing was the *rest* of her life.

The divorce agreement for Carrie was that she could reclaim Todd once she had stabilized herself; that was to be some time coming. In the meantime, she met a man whose wife had died recently and soon moved in with him. She's now convinced that he was only looking for someone to distract him from his grief, someone to be miserable with, but since she was herself at low ebb, she stayed with him three years even though he was constantly seeing other women. Perhaps she was punishing herself. "I felt I was a horrible person for leaving my husband and I was getting what I deserved."

At this time, Vincent was a teaching assistant living with a student who he knew was wrong for him. He and Carrie, who were already acquainted, started seeing more of each other on campus and within two weeks they were living together. Two years later they decided to marry, despite the predictions of friends that they wouldn't last six months once they made it legal.

Their friends' arguments had merit. All they had to do was look around and see that few marriages were working. Experience had taught them that you can't love and grow if you feel permanently locked in. But this was a commitment Vincent and Carrie were mature enough to accept. Vincent explained for both of them: "It is an announcement to everyone who means something to you that this is *the* person for you. We were letting other people know what expectations they should have of us and what expectations we had of each other." When the truth is told, they felt some pressure to marry for the reason stated by a friend of mine, who finally married her constant companion: "The attitude still exists that married couples know they're more accepted than people who live together."

Carrie and Vincent had a big wedding conducted outdoors in a woodland setting, complete with rabbi and parents and Carrie's son, Todd, whom she had reclaimed from her first husband. Vincent wanted everybody there so they could see for themselves that he and Carrie were taking a serious step. He feels that if you don't marry you are leaving something vital out of the relationship. It runs much deeper than any legal ritual. They both believe marriage is the best possible chance for growing into intimacy and for establishing absolute trust.

For Carrie, it had an extra dimension: "I was telling my child that this was how it was going to be and that he could count on stability. We were also saying to my parents, 'You don't have to worry that I am going flying off into the sunset anymore. I am not going to self-destruct.' It was a celebration of the fact that we were going to stay together."

Carrie and Vincent feel their marriage has made them freer. It has opened up many more options in their lives and they have discovered values that bind them closer together. The bonus in their life has been the significance of marriage for Todd, who is now eleven years old. "He had been very disillusioned," Carrie told me. "He was hurt when his father and I broke up and he also saw his father break up with his second wife. He saw me go through some impermanent relationships. Only lately is he feeling better about things. Only now does he feel secure."

Vincent and Carrie talk about having their own children but it isn't imperative. In fact, it's impractical for the time being. Their immediate concerns are how they are going to earn more money and whether or not they should move away from Los Angeles. Vincent believes there's a teaching or research job for him somewhere and right now Carrie is drifting and undecided. She is studying philology, has written some short stories, and considers being a writer, even though she thinks it's a little late to be starting at the bottom. But in their lives there is always room for new goals, no matter how fanciful. Vincent says: "In spite of the question marks in our lives, we've managed against all the odds to come emotionally together. We are calm and serene and one way or the other we have survived and will continue to."

Even though their three-year marriage has brought them little financial security, Carrie, in particular, feels very secure within herself. She used to worry about other women and about how long she and Vincent would last. Vincent assures her she never has any reason to worry and it matters very much to him that she examines what they have together. Marriage, he says, is a way of showing you don't intend to cheat on your partner. For him, their marriage has meant that the future doesn't seem so vague anymore. Carrie also noticed the difference marriage made with her parents, who treat them with respect now and take them seriously. Before, they thought Vincent was merely the current man in her life. Now with a wedding band on her finger, the men on campus and at the grocery store where she works have stopped making advances. It pleases Carrie that a wedding ring is still respected.

It is interesting to me that Carrie and Vincent, with all their emotional and sexual experiences, have a traditional monogamous marriage. And it surprises me that they are the couple who impressed me most deeply with their case for fidelity, and that they should come from the city of Los Angeles, otherwise known as Babylon. Out of their painfully won experience has come a personal acceptance of the fact that trust and intimacy come only with faithfulness. They don't understand people who think it is impossible to be hurt by infidelity. They tried open sexual relationships before they married but Carrie feels that such arrangements are inherently false. Even if you don't love the person it's destructive, because he or she desires someone more than you. These are their simple truths about lasting relationships, yet people keep looking for more complicated reasoning. Carrie says: "Some people don't trust how they feel, so they run around to an authority who tells them if it's okay to feel the way they do and then he hands out some formula. You don't need a guru to know if you're feeling happy. We'll be happy if we stop interfering with our natural instincts and values. But unfortunately happiness has been reduced to the intensity of sensation."

Vincent can't understand people who throw themselves away by trying to experience *all*. He doesn't even know what *all* is. But sex, money, and status are the more obvious manifestations. "There are still the intellectual aspects of a life. I have other curiosities and expectations and they are things I know I can obtain. I know my intellectual life can be unlimited and it isn't concentrated on the big orgasm. I don't have time for intense affairs because they would drown me. If I have to choose, I won't choose cheap sensations. I want to understand what it is to be a human being."

If monogamy is the answer, I ask them, why do so many people insist that it is an impossible life-style that stunts personal growth? There is no hesitation in either of their replies. Multiple sexual relationships may open up new interests, but if you believe it is a worthy goal to want to move on toward spiritual and intellectual pursuits, you can't stay trapped on the sexual level. Being as intimate as possible with one person is as fulfilling as knowing dozens of people. "I don't think fidelity is all that unnatural," Carrie says. "And I was born in Los Angeles, where it supposedly doesn't exist. I know there is a craziness that is centered in Hollywood but I think it's a fantasy fed by people who move here from places like Wisconsin."

Vincent expands: "I don't know if it's the life-style of the stars, but Hollywood seems to offer the stereotype of romance and thrills, and when it goes sour you simply cast yourself in a new romance. When a new romance is at its peak, it's very exciting and it's as addictive as heroin—and it doesn't last. You get used to the high and you use the other person to get it. It's like going around saying, 'How would you like to be my latest fix?'"

Vincent and Carrie have floundered themselves but they know clearly now what is important to them. For Carrie, no one is as intellectually stimulating as Vincent. For him, she is the only person he can say anything to and have it completely understood. They are in accord with each other's values and wishes but they have by no means absorbed each other's individuality. He is theoretical and concerned with the mysteries of life. She is more practical and suggests that this may be the nature of women—being more tied to the earth. They have their disagreements and times when something is in the air and they don't talk. If it seems an important problem is submerged, one will raise the issue and it's usually resolved in a manner both can accept.

Later, when we are driving along the freeway in their rusted car to return some library books, Vincent says he is tired of hearing how marriage doesn't work anymore, tired of hearing people pejoratively labeled old-fashioned and out of step with the cultural revolution because they believe in honesty and responsibility, even at the cost of some personal satisfaction.

Sex is just as important to Carrie and Vincent as anyone else, but they don't think they are martyrs or their lives are stunted because their orgasms aren't always the biggest and the best. For them, the essential task is to know yourself and it is life-enhancing to know another person almost as well. It is important to understand that we come alone into the world and will leave it the same way. What makes the interval worthwhile is to choose our companions along the way with great care, and to accept that a betrayal of them is also a betrayal of self. Carrie and Vincent accept security and peace on a day-to-day basis over momentary excitement, and it has nothing to do with religion or culturally imposed morality. They say these values are stamped into the human psyche.

Living within the shadow of Hollywood, Vincent and Carrie have read the neon messages of lust but have chosen a different life. We have entered that part of the city where the women walking by are wearing boots that are probably worth more than Carrie and Vincent's car, but on the hill, where the weeds overgrow their broken house, they're shaping a future that includes an eleven-year-old boy who knows he's going to be coming home to the same people every day. From now on.

The spirit of living well *from now on* permeates the life of June, who married Hartley after his first marriage, which lasted sixteen years and was misery all the way. She announces proudly: "I am the best thing that happened to him!" They are as enthusiastically confident in their marriage as Carrie and Vincent are, and their values are similar. But all stories are different and this one takes place in Philadelphia, a bewildering city where genealogy and propriety really count, but the reality is unsafe streets and racial paranoia.

It is June's first marriage but she's probably more knowledgeable than most about the horrors of some marriages and the risks of the "second time around" because she has spent years researching and writing about them. She never wanted a husband and when she did marry at thirty-three, it was as much of a surprise to her as it was to her friends, who saw her as a self-sufficient career woman. Certainly, she felt, the current disintegration of love and vows in society was no promotion for getting married, and Hartley had a more difficult time adjusting to a second life than Carrie and Vincent. The younger couples were more resilient, and they had both experimented with different life-styles.

Hartley took monogamy to the limits. Even when his marriage became intolerable, he never looked around for other possibilities. He was absolutely married, and he never expected a chance for happiness with anyone else, and he was never unfaithful. He simply didn't come home until he knew his wife Myrna and the children were in bed.

Carrie and Vincent recognized the mistakes of their first marriages and believed in their right to a new life. This idea was unthinkable to Hartley when he was married to Myrna. He was reared strictly on the exhortation that marriage lasted until death. So when the seemingly impossible happened and he moved in with June, his new lover had to deal with his guilt and pain—something that Carrie never had to face. On top of this June had to watch as Hartley's ex-wife, enraged when he wouldn't suffer her tirades anymore, retaliated by speaking against him to his four children. Two of them turned their backs on him. This was precisely the kind of marital untidiness June had determined to avoid, even at the cost of never having a husband.

When Carrie married at eighteen, June was already establishing herself in a writing career and had long before adjusted to the fact that she was unpopular with men through all the rejections by boys in her high school; she never expected a man to play any major role in her personal life. She realized early what a lot of girls around her didn't: you can find your talent and make it take you as far as you can go and self-worth, not prettiness, has everything to do with it. She dated but had no great love affairs. There were no insurmountable moral scruples but she knew, without necessarily having to go through it, that a series of liaisons would leave her disappointed and empty. In her early days as a writer she was always in the company of men, all of them married, and affairs weren't her style. But she had many casual friends because she is zany, always eager for a laugh and the unexpected. Her plain-but-nice appearance, which never won her many compliments, was unimportant compared to her sympathetic interest in people and a certain cachet that accrues when you have a career that puts you in the public eye. She was independent and content and not at all interested when a young woman in her office kept insisting she should meet her uncle, who had recently separated. June remembers thinking: "Times may be tough but they're not *that* tough!"

The girl persisted and June, who describes herself as a "lunatic" and a "crazy," invited him to some weird event involving hippies and a light show. When he agreed to this somewhat unusual invitation, she thought to herself that he couldn't be all that bad. But on the night of the date, she was irritable because she had to get up early, and besides, what was she doing with a blind date anyway? Hartley claims he knew from the beginning that June was going to be important to him. Within months after their first meeting, Hartley and June moved into a condominium in Center City. It would take two years for his divorce to become final so "we decided to make up a story for his children," June says, "because we didn't want them to think we were living in sin." The fable was that it was Hartley's apartment and June was just helping him to redecorate.

It was during these months together that Hartley gradually unburdened himself of the disturbing details of his marriage, which he had known from the start was unrealistic. He blames himself because it should never have taken place. He calls it "the classic case of the knight rescuing the maiden."

"Myrna was terribly beaten by her father, who was an evil son of a bitch. I got caught up. I was a college graduate and she was nothing. My motives were unrealistically romantic. I decided I had to save her. She didn't want to marry me. It was my own aggressiveness that led to the marriage. I had no previous relations with women and I was the virgin hero who was going to rescue this woman."

Hartley referred to Myrna as a "woman" but she was a beaten teenager who had never done anything to remove herself from her wretched circumstances. It should have come as no surprise to him that she became almost totally dependent on her husband. But he honestly believed in the beginning that he could help her become an independent person who could develop whatever talents had been crushed by her upbringing. He insisted that she go to university and develop her mind and outside interests. But she wanted to stay indoors just as her mother had done, and let Hartley take care of all her needs. She immediately became pregnant, which Hartley sees now as a deliberate ploy so she wouldn't have to deal with going to university, as he wanted. Three more pregnancies followed and it infuriated him. Myrna made sure she remained dependent on him and kept him locked to her because of the children.

Hartley retaliated by leaving for work at seven in the morning and coming home at midnight. I asked him what effect this had on his children and he made no apologies for the chaos that ensued. Sundays, his one day with the children, were hectic because he took them all over the place. If, during the week, he did come home early—but not before dinner was finished—he would concentrate on helping them with their homework. The marriage was falling apart and even the youngest children sensed it. He says, with more dismay than bitterness, that Myrna was exactly like her mother—a martyr through and through. "She saw me as her father, who was always pushing her around physically. I guess I *was* pushing her around by insisting that she make something of herself. She had no affection for me, ever. She just wanted security but she didn't want to be with me physically."

During their sixteenth year together, Hartley felt like a destroyed man. He couldn't go on living like this, yet a puritanical notion informed him that he had brought this life down on his own head and he would have to stick by it. His only hope for a change in his life seemed to be through professional help so he could understand himself and his wife's side of the story a little better. He went to a marriage counselor for eighteen months before he finally saw some light.

After persuading Myrna to come to the counselor with him a few times, Hartley was shocked by what she said to them. "She had a totally other view of me. I thought I was helping her when I urged her to go to university at night and offered to look after the children. *She* thought I considered her deficient. It was insoluble. We had nothing in common but four kids. What I had to come to understand was that Myrna enjoyed her dependent life and I would have to provide it, but there was no way in the world I could adjust to that." During one of his sessions alone, Hartley's therapist put all the cards on the table. Why was Hartley still coming to see him? He either had to alter all his expectations and accept his wife as a retiring, domestic, introverted woman, or he had to leave her. His therapist told him *somebody* had to survive this disaster. This gave him the courage.

"She was calm when I said I was leaving her. I packed my things and drove off. I went to a motel for a while and then I lived all sorts of places. I'd go to work, then to an athletic club until it closed and then to dinner alone, which would carry me until about eleven at night. I would find some friends I could stay up with, and talk until early in the morning. Sometimes they let me sleep over. You really need that sort of help for a short time. You become quite ingenious about finding places where you can stay overnight so you can avoid going back to a motel." It was at this juncture that Hartley and June met. He was a tired, aimless, sexless man who had not dated for six months.

As for June, the careerist who had always managed to convey, on the surface at least, the blessedness of single life, she was getting older and feeling that some people regarded her as *peculiar*. Although she and Hartley began to see each other often, both conveyed the distinct message that they didn't need anybody. Hartley had resolved that he would not make the mistake of some divorced men who marry a version of their first wives, but it soon became apparent that June could be the woman he should have met in the first place. She was confident of her view of the world and she was living the way she wanted to. June liked the fact that Hartley invited her to do such unglamorous things as go bicycle riding. They were pleased to learn they shared the same political and social point of view. (This has undoubtedly contributed to the peacefulness of their household. Both are eager anytime for a debate on a controversial subject.) He also didn't try to push her into bed. When they did make love months later, they embraced as mature lovers, not as figments of a romantic imagination. A down-to-earth sense of reality is the hallmark of their life together.

Listening to Hartley talk, I pick up on the fact that he has no illusions about his personality, which can be pedantic and conservative, although he likes to point out that he was for women's liberation long before so-called liberals so noisily took up the cause. He is balding and a little overweight from success. His manufacturing business is thriving and he enjoys the commuter club car that takes him in and out of Philadelphia several times a week solidifying contracts. He is forty-nine, only five years older than June, but when he's weary he seems almost an old man. June appears much younger by comparison, perhaps because she has no marital battle scars.

June's declaration that she was the best thing that happened to Hartley is unquestionably true. Hartley says she was literally his salvation. Still, he was wary of her for a while. Hartley *needed* evidence that June would continue to be independent, to earn her own living. If this was so, he knew they would have a tremendously good relationship. He was constantly looking for any sign of incipient dependence in her.

June has an exuberant sense of humor and I doubt if she showed Hartley her bank account. She made this perfectly clear: "I didn't want to quit my job. I liked my life. I liked my cooking and I was not interested in changing or having to adapt my ways to his." She discovered she didn't have to change at all and she had the added dimension of constant support. When she was working on a difficult piece of writing, Hartley was her sounding board. Although she always made up her own mind, he would give his honest opinion when she asked for it—and he kept the coffee coming.

Hartley was generous with financial support for his children and former wife and it was wishful thinking on his part that June would not have to become involved in his family situation. But she was willing and considered it inevitable. She became a part of the statistics she often uses in her writing. (According to the U. S. National Center for Health Statistics, nearly one million children under the age of eighteen see a parent remarry, and well over a half million adults suddenly find themselves in the stepparent role.) Soon after their marriage, Hartley's teenaged son stalked out on his mother and moved in with them. He arrived in a hostile, revengeful mood, determined to make somebody pay for the fact that his family was split. June says: "I just kept trying to talk to him and telling myself that he was charming in spite of his attempts to be so miserable. Eventually we had a great time. We grew to love each other and he stayed with us for three years." His other son respects her and telephones often. Of his two daughters, Hartley says: "They are very much like their mother and loyal to her. We have minimal contact."

Children who are used as pawns, and malice that is difficult to resolve, are the end products of many divorces. June is a generous woman who was willing to endure a great deal during the early part of their marriage. Her confidence and self-image are such that she was determined that her happiness and Hartley's would not be threatened by the spitefulness of someone else. The fact that she earns a good salary and has prestige makes a great difference: "If I want a dress I go out and buy it. Hartley spends his money on his family and that's the way I think it should be."

June, who is slim and agile, tends to curl into various positions on the couch while Hartley sits a little stiffly in full suit. When he talks about June, he visibly relaxes and his expression is serene. The reason he has talked so long about his first marriage, he explains, is to show the absolute contrast with his second marriage. He has made no mistake this time. He is lavish with his words of admiration for June and it is fine to witness the interplay between them and see how much June relishes his attentions. "We are emotionally intertwined," she says. "He's home at night because he wants to be with me. Our favorite companions are each other. He tells me everything and we talk incessantly and we fight about what I am saying in my articles."

June says that monogamy works unless you're the kind of person who doesn't have deep feelings. She is aware of sex as sport but it never appealed to her. Before she could become intimate with a man, she needed to feel totally relaxed and to trust him. Hartley has been the only man who has made her feel that way. She says she can do without sex if necessary and the world wouldn't come to an end. Human relationships, social reform, and her career have always been important. She feels fortunate that her life does not revolve around sexual tension and its satisfaction. When she and Hartley make love, it is beautiful; if it doesn't happen for a while, she doesn't worry.

Hartley says he could not live with the guilt of infidelity. In fact, it would be worse than guilt; it would be "depravity. I truly believe and accept the fact that June is my perfect mate, intellectually and sexually, and I don't seek or want any other woman." June says she doesn't concern herself about Hartley meeting another woman, but if he did it would destroy her.

They talk of some people they see around them who seem not to have plumbed the depths of marriage or developed the extraordinary intimacy that is possible. "We recently went to a party," June says, "where the men were making nasty cracks about their wives and telling jokes about them and the women were saying, 'What do you expect from a husband? They're all alike.' It seems they've got their kids and their houses and an investment that keeps them together, but they don't have true closeness and they aren't each other's best friend. This seems so common. Hartley is the only one I tell my secrets to, but there is a core of my private self that I maintain. I don't feel every single detail or thought that crosses my mind must be imparted to him."

I ask June how she feels about being a second wife. The

connotations of being *second* can be dangerous to the spirit. The letters written to Dear Abby constantly smart with the jealousies of the new wife: the deceased wife's portrait which has never been removed from the mantelpiece; the telephone call from the former wife whose furnace has broken down again, the son or daughter from the previous marriage who arrives at the father's house on Saturday, looks at the other woman, and demands: "Is *she* going to be with us?"

June has the answer. "If Hartley were a widower and had been wildly happy with his wife and I was the second, I don't know if I could take it. It would upset me if there were the ghost of a wife. But I feel that I am Hartley's first love and that he is my first love. That other marriage didn't count."

Before he met Naomi, Arnold thought he knew exactly the kind of life he was going to lead—a very solitary one. He bought a ramshackle house near a deer reserve outside a prairie city in Canada. He was going to repair the house himself and there he would sit with his violins and commune with nature and God. He is a master violinist; he has played with many symphony orchestras and the beauty of the music he creates has been solace enough when everything else has gone wrong. And there was plenty of that, with two ex-wives and six children, and so many memories of good times and bad. His experiences during his sixty years had made him think that he should be alone.

I walked down the path to Arnold's place, brushing against the tangled hedges, hoping for a glimpse of some of the deer behind the high fence. I was greeted by a very distinguished-looking man, tall and thin, with long gray hair and a perfect goatee. He has had his periods of frail health and there are signs of it, but this impression is quickly replaced by the sensation of a serenity and a joyfulness. It sets him apart from some men of his age who seem older and bewildered by the rapid changes in a world they thought they knew. He introduces me to the source of his well-being: Naomi, his third wife. She was a totally unexpected addition to the theme he had planned for his remaining years. They were married a year ago and he tells me, in an unselfconscious burst of sentiment, that he was given another chance late in life when he finally found his "ideal woman." Naomi flushes with pleasure.

She seems to fit the biblical image of her name. She is a woman strong in her own mind, but she makes it clear that Arnold is the head of their house and she will follow. Plain and unassuming, she is also an accomplished musician—his equal, he insists, although she is eighteen years younger than he is. Together the two of them seem as harmonious as their finely tuned instruments. Their house retains the atmosphere of a cottage that isn't finished. What was likely a bedroom has become a temporary music room. Someday they would like to attach a little studio to the house, but that will come in its time because Arnold wants to accomplish this with his own hands.

Naomi had known of Arnold for a long time because she sometimes played oboe with the Boston Symphony, of which he was a member for twenty-four years. From 1965, they moved in the same traveling music circle but since they were both married to someone else he did not pay much attention to her. When Noami was two years divorced and Arnold had been separated for several years from his second wife, they found themselves playing together once more in the same orchestra. Neither of them was interested in trying marriage again. Each had once believed that marriage was forever and both felt a sense of failure because they had not achieved lasting unity with their partners.

Naomi was "doing all right" at the time, emotionally and socially, and Arnold simply wanted no more confusion. They were not especially withdrawn people and music filled any voids. But still, here they were, sitting on the same stages night after night, so Arnold began to talk to her and invite her to dinner; she was very flattered. Then their meetings became more frequent and personal during six months on the road and at the end of the tour they were quietly married.

During that time, Naomi had to make a major mental adjustment because she had to stop associating marriage with eventual failure. Gradually she accepted the idea that divorce is the only alternative when two people make each other miserable and neither is willing, nor perhaps able, to do anything about it. She realized that many people are not properly matched and there is no sense in their trying to stay together when the marriage turns bitter and brings out the worst in them. Her divorce was not amicable, but then relatively few are. There were never-ending disputes over money and when the dust settled, she had her freedom and an ulcer.

Naomi's answer to why she married again is simple: "Because I was very much in love with Arnold in a spiritual sense and in the real sense." Arnold says: "I had never known a woman like her. She helped me reach that final stage of maturity where I found what I was looking for and was prepared to accommodate myself to the bumps in the road."

Naomi has two daughters from her first marriage, which lasted eighteen years, and Arnold's children range in age from twelve to thirty-four years. His first marriage ended after eleven years and his second after twenty. Their various children have occupied much of their one year together, but it has not unduly disturbed their peace with each other. Naomi's teenaged daughter has been with them since their marriage and Arnold's fourteen-year-old daughter has spent varying periods of time with them. His twelve-year-old son also came for a summer. Arnold has always been exasperated by his inability to control children, but Naomi tends to smooth the problem over. In fact, she says he has become quite patient with them and this is because Arnold has newly developed a willingness to try to understand and communicate with her daughter. He started by encouraging her in what has now become a family ritual: after dinner she reads to them from a book they have all chosen and then they play cards. Small things such as this have drawn them closer. "She has been with me for a long time," Naomi reminds Arnold, "and you have been very good and mature about it." Arnold smiles and concedes in a rather formal voice that the child does appear to be accepting responsibility and acknowledging that someone exists in the world besides herself. But it's such a trivial annoyance, Naomi says. "Think what it must be like when children deliberately try to ruin their parents' new marriages?"

While Naomi says that Arnold has shown more kindness and patience toward her daughter than most men would for another's child, he is rather harsh when he speaks of the times his own teenaged daughter has visited. "It didn't work out," he says brusquely. "She had no desire to make a home with us. She wanted to go her own way." He concedes that she's more even-tempered now that she has a job. It is obvious they have willingly opened their lives and their small home to the comings and goings of children from three different partners. There may be impatience occasionally but remarkably little hostility.

Arnold pointed out that marriage involves children and the shaping of their personalities and no matter what happens to you and your spouse, the children remain with you—even if only in the mind. He expected his first marriage to be his last and he is not inclined to refer to past failures. He spoke of his first wife only briefly. They married when they were both in the Army, and once they shed their uniforms and the discipline, they seemed strangers in each other's eyes. Arnold turned immediately to music, which was alien to her, and it eventually proved fatal to the marriage. Of his second marriage, he remarked: "It didn't work out for all sorts of reasons. And that's that." Neither of them believes there is any benefit in talking of their former spouses. Naomi would only say that she and her first husband were music students and he and their families had pressured her into marriage. Her mistake was a common one, she says. "People marry too young."

Apart from their music, Arnold and Naomi share their

belief in God. Arnold says with conviction: "All life and love comes from God and we are fortunate to share that gift. I discovered my former wives had no basic beliefs. They believed God had little to do with them while I believe it is the whole basis of life." The intimacy of marriage and the sharing of its joys and sorrows rest on a foundation far stronger than something like fate, or the random selection of a mate who very much enthralled you at one stage of your life.

They believe in monogamy although they are aware of the options available to married couples. They feel that open relationships must lead eventually to disaster; in these circumstances, people really can't help each other, which is the tremendous strength of a loyal marriage. Arnold says: "It seems unlikely to me that you can have commitment without fidelity. You destroy many things, such as complete trust and being able to communicate with the other person. We exist because Naomi is for me and I am for her. Commitment with reservations is impossible." Complete trust, Naomi says, is what allows people to develop their full human potential. Arnold feels he is proof of that. Since their marriage, he finds himself less testy and more generous with his colleagues and less inclined to think things will go wrong.

Before I go, Arnold and Naomi speak of their music and their shared language is both poetical and spiritual. They describe how pleasantly aware they are of each other's presence when they are playing together in the symphony. They tell of how, when the music is done, they are alone with their moment of self-judgment. It is a moment when each of them wonders how much closer to perfection he or she might get the next time they perform—and this constant quest to be better seems to me to have extended into and enhanced all aspects of Arnold and Naomi's life.

6

Love Thy Neighbor
Open Marriages

A young California man, a blithe spirit if I ever met one, told me he did not believe in jealousy. "Like, you know, it's just cultural." But jealousy really was the rub in California, where I came across men and women having joyously liberating sex with others and at the same time living committed lives with their partners. The main question, I asked myself as I took a taxi to Irene's house outside of Los Angeles, was how can anyone hold such mutually exclusive ideas in their head at the same time? I thought an answer could be found with couples who live in a successful open marriage.

When I arrived at Irene's, she was dealing with a service person fixing all sorts of window screens and doors, and immediately tried to talk to me about her sex life. All the while she kept an eye on the clock for an appointment she had to discuss an awareness workshop for executives who have not developed the "art of relating." Irene is in her forties, tall and very tanned. She wore no makeup and her blonde-and-gray-streaked hair was casually tossed over her shoulders. She was very friendly, talkative, and embarrassingly energetic to someone as sedentary as I.

She and her husband, Graham, forty-five, who is a management consultant, sometimes are guest speakers at sex and marriage therapy courses. Irene has always been an enthusiastic volunteer, working for civil rights and the women's movement, licking envelopes at the local political level. I asked her, as she was warming some breakfast rolls for me in the microwave oven, to open the conversation at any point she liked. She proceeded to talk about a growth center she is involved with that researches couples in sexually open marriages. These people, she explained, were into swinging, wife-swapping, and three-person encounters. She tells me she is impressed by these couples' commitment to communication. Both she and Graham have experience with humanistic psychology with its emphasis on being direct and totally honest, which can also be very painful for some.

Eventually Irene took me into her early time with Graham. For the first fifteen years of their marriage she was the traditional wife and mother, devoting most of her time to raising five sensitive and creative children, and giving support to her husband as he quickly advanced in his career. (Both Irene and Graham travel frequently and the reason I was not interviewing them together was that he was out of town.) In 1970, something very important happened to Irene which led her to fall back on the totally honest principles of humanistic psychology. As a homemaker and an aware citizen, she became concerned with civil rights, volunteered at the grass-roots level, moved up into the hierarchy of an organization, and began traveling to training sessions. Until then she had been, in her mind, just a wife and mother.

"Suddenly I was a powerful person within the movement. I got a lot of attention from men and I really got scared."

It had never happened before, but Irene became sexually involved with a man during an out-of-town weekend seminar. She only alluded to this incident but later her husband spoke very openly about it. He told me that she felt guilty after this weekend and had to tell him about it because she had never been dishonest with him before. She felt, under the circumstances, that he should have the choice of doing the same thing. The long hurtful conversation resulted in a mutual decision to open their marriage sexually. They both remember that they were shocked, scared, and intrigued by the very thought of it.

"We talked into the night," Irene recalls. "We felt our relationship should be absolutely primary, but we decided to have outside relationships that might include sexual experiences. We set up a lot of rules. The important one was that our relationship comes first. When we started out on this new basis, we took very small steps. We kept checking back on how we were feeling and whether we were hurting each other or other people. One rule was that we would never be with anyone else during times when we could be available to each other. So what we do is travel separately and relate sexually to others."

In fact, Irene says, if their thinking had not radically altered, they might have divorced because of her initial act of infidelity. The reason their open arrangement works, she says, is that they are honest and their primary commitment is to each other. Although Irene initiated the sexual experiment, she found it very frightening because it gave her a new sense of independence, and also an intimation of the possible loss of a life she had been comfortable with. She had always seen herself as a less strong person than her husband. With the open marriage, she became stronger and Graham began to explore the gentler aspects of his personality. He had leaned too heavily on the macho side before. She says they have found an open marriage to be a very "affirming" process. But, she adds, they are far more cautious than other people who enter into such arrangements.

Irene finds it easier than Graham to approach people and develop an instant rapport. She doesn't go to bars and pick up men, but she says she is "free to be me" when she is on her out-of-town trips. She doesn't believe that she and Graham are especially promiscuous. They expect their marriage to endure. "I am not looking for a substitute or a new husband. No matter what happened, I could not imagine that I'd ever marry again. Our marriage is so special that I'm not sure I could try again."

Despite the long nights of confidences and reassurances that characterize some open marriages, I couldn't help but wonder about moments of aloneness. Is it easier when you know nothing or when you know every single detail? Irene and Graham have worked it out so that no one is waiting at home for the other's return. They arrange it so they don't see any particular person too much. Some of their partners are married and some are also in open relationships. Irene tends to short-term sexual relationships with younger men. Often her partners become friends and then the sex stops. Which leads me to a question: If the purpose of open marriage is to explore and widen personal relationships to the fullest extent, why is sex withdrawn from the lovers who become friends? I suspect that Irene is not prepared for the risk of an emotional involvement that would threaten her marriage.

Monogamy, which Graham and Irene once knew so well, is relatively unrealistic, Irene says. "Sexuality has messed up so many people. There are many limitations with monogamy. I've never had a homosexual liaison but some of my friends are into that. I never say never to anything anymore. I believe there are people who are monogamous and they are okay with that. Graham and I have said we'll go back to that if one of us is hurting, but I don't think we will. Our outside sexual activity has diminished but it's important to have the options."

So far, outside partners are kept strictly away from Graham and Irene's family and home, but this is becoming an issue which worries Irene because Graham has suggested bringing their partners into their lives. To her, this smacks of "swinging," which she hates. It's too much like some people she knows who publicly date their lovers.

I ask Irene how they deal with the return from an out-of-town trip where they may have been sexually involved with another man or woman. Irene says: "I make a point of meeting Graham at the airport and sometimes we go to the beach and talk about how his trip has been. One of the questions will be if he met someone. It's fine to ask that and I get a straight answer. I think a little of the tension of relationships has to do with the forbidden-fruit aspect of outside sex. Well, it's not forbidden in our relationship and it's not that big a number."

Graham has a much freer attitude about sex than she has, Irene says, and there is the slight possibility that things can go too far. She has heard what other people do, and says flatly: "I don't want to watch Graham have sex with someone else. I can handle what we're doing now and I consider it enriching. But I see people start out on an open relationship and it's really the first step to divorce." Irene tells me she and Graham had a good marriage and a good sex life before they opened their possibilities. As I leave, she emphasizes something she told me earlier: "One of our commitments is that if our marriage gets into trouble we will not do this anymore."

In his office where he works as a successful management consultant, Graham sits with his feet up on his desk appearing to be a very casual person, though I soon learn that he is not. He regards me sternly and demands to know how I am going to use the information I have gathered. He is tall and slim with a luxurious beard and it is easy to visualize the attractiveness he has for his wife and for other women. We begin safely enough talking about his children. "I have been most concerned with giving them the greatest possible leeway to make decisions for themselves. That requires being available so they can have the benefit of our point of view. I don't think that permissiveness means you aren't available. You may need to be more available than when you have a tight family structure." As he continued to talk in this manner, I kept trying to figure out how he let a woman know that he was available for an expanded relationship. I also found that while Irene was gutsy, thought-provoking, and exotic—possibly even shy— Graham seemed upright, judgmental, and rather aggressively sure of himself in sexual matters. This may be his reaction to the embarrassment he still feels about the fact that he and

Irene hadn't a single notion about what marriage would be like when they started out. "This bothers me really because I merely went through stages. I went to school. I went to college. I married and I had kids. I did all those things because that's what you did. I thought marriage involved permanence. I didn't think of it as temporary or as a trial."

In the beginning, which was 19 years ago, Graham and Irene did what everyone else was doing: they carved out spheres of influence. Irene was the authority on children and he was to have a successful career. Long before women's liberation came along, he says he was sharing some of the domestic chores provided they did not interfere with his business advancement. He also believed that Irene was too intelligent, too vital, not to have a full-time career of her own someday. Money was never a problem. She had an inheritance and he earned a good salary. There was never any question of his or her money; the bank account was joint. In fact, they were so easy about money and so sure of each other's tastes that Irene bought their house while he was away for a weekend. "She made the decision but if I didn't like it we would have gotten out of the deal. But it was fine with me." Decisions about the house, their careers, and the raising of the children have been relatively simple for them because they both want the same things. True, Irene's suggestion to open their marriage was uncharacteristic but she seemed to deem it necessary and Graham was willing to go along.

"I thought it was really exciting that she suddenly had this perception about another way to live. It had never been on the agenda. The way it had been going she was less adventuresome. She seemed to have more worries. I don't think we ever talked about having sex with other people before that weekend. My intellectual response was 'That's terrific!' But I remember being surprised at how much I experienced unsettling emotions. When she came back from her weekend and we started to talk about sexual activity, I wouldn't say I was jealous on any conscious level but I was quite concerned to hear her be so explicit about what happened. Maybe I was a little concerned about what I could trust and what I couldn't."

They had always liked the idea of having close, platonic relationships with the opposite sex, but only if they both knew these other people and were friends. Now they have to work out different limits to their outside relationships since sex may be involved. In fact, this concern with coming to understand each other's feelings and expectations delayed their first sexual encounters for quite some time. The important rule was that they have the right to expect the other to be absolutely candid. Graham, for instance, will describe the other woman, how he met her, why he was attracted to her, and what sexual behavior they engaged in. Irene has the right to decide if she feels "comfortable" with the situation. If she ever feels hurt or threatened or angry, Graham has to end the liaison. It works both ways.

Still, the early years of open marriage were far from painless. Before they worked out a formula for not getting too involved, Graham had a relationship in which he hurt a woman rather badly. Perhaps he had not made it clear that his marriage would always come first. "In the beginning, what we found the scariest were relationships of great intimacy where someone else might come to play a special role. We were worried that a perfect person might come along and destroy our marriage." They are certainly testing their marriage to the limits and it has held, but it is a kind of living on the edge that very few people could tolerate. Graham and Irene live with the whole truth and nothing but. Many women assume adultery will occur sometime in their relationship but there are time-honored ways of coping with it. Some women say: "What I don't know won't hurt me." Others say: "I knew what was going on but I waited around until he came to his senses." Truth does not necessarily set you free; sometimes it hurts like hell.

Graham conveys a certain sense of superiority that he and Irene are not the typical middle-aged married couple. In their script there is no role for the "betrayed one" or the "sinner." This has loosened their sexual relations with each other. "It's easy," Graham says, "to talk about what we like sexually. We are more explicit and more adventuresome. We talk about what it's like with other people. It has made us more sexually attractive to each other and it has confirmed for both of us that people find us attractive." Graham says they have never looked back. He has never felt their decision was a mistake. Plainly speaking, he would have missed a lot in his life. The single regret is that they didn't know of these possibilities sooner.

There is a calm frankness and an aura of a rather extraordinary emotional maturity in their marriage, but I felt a gap in their thinking about the next stage of their lives. Irene suggested she wouldn't mind tapering off, that she has no interest in advanced forms of sexual experimentation. She doesn't want to share Graham with the neighborhood and she doesn't want to get to know his women. She isn't interested in trying a homosexual relationship even though she knows some liberated women see this as the logical next step in getting to know all about themselves.

But Graham's idea is different. "For myself, I wouldn't mind trying to incorporate into our joint lives some of the people we are involved with. I don't see anything wrong in involving the woman I'm with in the relationship I have with my wife. Of course I wouldn't want to have to decide some evening which one to sleep with. It might be possible that Irene's sexual partner might become a friend of mine and the three of us might spend an evening over dinner. I'm not really clear that there is anything I would rule out in advance, or that I wouldn't consider doing."

Some of this is fantasy, though, because Graham says in the next breath that he would not do anything to cause Irene unhappiness. "She doesn't have to writhe in agony to let me know she's unhappy. She'd just have to mention it and I would stop." I am stopped here to wonder how, after years of sexual freedom, Graham or Irene suddenly announces that it's over, and it's home to monogamy? How would this be achieved? Well, they'd just cut it out, he guesses. "Quite frankly, once you get past the initial fascination, the sexual aspect isn't *that* great."

Hannah and Grant, who are in their middle thirties, still have difficulties in their open relationship. Grant likes to be spontaneous, to act on the spur of the moment, which often gets him into trouble. He has actually walked out of parties with an attractive woman on his arm, leaving Hannah to go home to bed alone. Hannah considers herself sexually liberated but, damn it, not so liberated that it doesn't hurt sometimes. Still, open sexuality is what is best for them.

A truly great place to be in San Francisco is a Victorian house. Hannah and Grant occupy half of one in an ethnically mixed neighborhood with enough street fighters to add tension to their daily lives. When I met them, they were in their big white kitchen preparing a lunch of cheese and bread and white wine. Hannah is tanned, slim, and short and has long frizzy hair. She is wearing a denim skirt, mini length, and as she moves about the kitchen, bending over this or that, she shows a lot of dainty underwear. Grant's occasional belches are so friendly you almost want to join in. He is tall with long dark hair and a beard. They look attractive together and they know it. There is a stack of dirty dishes and Hannah explains that it took her a long time to learn not to worry about them. Grant sits with his big feet pressed against her belly. They say they had a big fight on the way home from marketing that morning and seriously considered calling off the interview. But argument is communication and the air is clear.

Hannah and Grant have been living together six years and do not intend to get married. Hannah has a bad taste in her mouth from her previous marriage. She married young and knew it was a mistake from the start but she stayed for eight years because she didn't know what else to do. Grant has never married and he doesn't like the sound of it.

Hannah and Grant's relationship is a seeming contradiction in terms: they are free and they are committed. Marriage counselors, psychologists, and experts who concern themselves with such matters have differing opinions about whether monogamy can survive in the twenty-first century. Some believe the relationship Hannah and Grant are developing will be very attractive and workable for more and more people in the future, but that is going to depend on how well people can control such basic human traits as jealousy, trust, and exclusivity. Grant and Hannah have established a home base where certain expectations are to be met. Beyond that they are as emotionally and sexually free from each other as the larks in the clear air.

While they are interested in each other's direction in life, Grant and Hannah are dedicated to their own personal pathways. There is not the oneness of feeling about children or the mutual goals required by marriage because these things do not figure at all in their lives. They are pleased with each other as individuals; as a couple I would say they are engaged in pursuits rather than a reckoned direction in life. This is what they are trying to escape from.

In a world that is indifferent and unfriendly outside of a close circle of friends, they believe in remaining together no matter what it takes. Being left would hurt them as much as it would anyone else. The things they want for themselves—being warm in bed when the other comes home, and being able to recognize and compensate for varying moods—are scarcely the hallmarks of a life-style any braver than the one we're used to. In spite of the exotic element in the way they live, it is continuity they desire, the sense of being able to rely on someone else for a few things, but probably not as many things as in a traditional marriage. They're young but they talk seriously of sudden death, which is very Californian. They say the earthquakes are coming for sure and probably sooner than

anyone realizes. Had I noticed the posh apartment building set
upon concrete stilts? The first good tremor and all those rich
people are going to fall out of there like sticks. In San
Francisco, people are fatalistic but also hopeful. Hannah and
Grant postulate that when the big quake comes they're going
to be visiting relatives in Minnesota. Then they laugh and
agree that this is the only rationale to have.

Hannah was raised in San Francisco and married at
eighteen for one reason only: the Air Force. She was working
as a secretary and the boy she was living with was a student.
When he was drafted they decided they would have to get
married so she could move to the base with him. She was just
out of high school and certainly not an adult. She says what
happened wasn't too surprising. Their first year of marriage
was good and the next seven years were bad. She discovered
early on that she and her husband had a tendency to get lazy
and take each other for granted. "I didn't have a chance to be
who I wanted to be," she told me. "We had no children because I didn't want any and after a while that became a source
of conflict. I gradually learned that it's often the men who become complacent and develop a nesting instinct." Grant, who
had no uneasiness listening to Hannah talk about her former
husband, suggested that men have flings and more of a chance
to find out who they are before they get married. Afterward
they buy the comforts and, yes, the servitude, and it is often
women who decide they want more. Grant believes this is an
inescapable pattern for people who marry before they're thirty
years old.

In the six years they've lived together developing an honest and open communication, Hannah and Grant have had to
tell a lot of lies. Grant lied to insurance companies and to em-
ployers because there is still discrimination against common-
law relationships. It's a stupid, bureaucratic fact of life when
the reality of their personal lives is that most of their friends
and relatives aren't married. Grant has never felt an urge to
marry but he believes in living with one woman at a time. If

she lasts a very long time, that's fine with him. Their way of viewing the world is identical and would be thought radical by many just a generation removed. Grant's parents consider their relationship illicit and cope by pretending they are married. He is the son of a minister from Philadelphia; his parents are in their sixties. His upbringing was straitlaced. Somewhere along the line he became determined that marriage was a deadening influence. He is also horrified by the legal and emotional nightmares when people split. By contrast, Hannah's mother is forty-nine and lives nearby with a man fifteen years her junior. Grant calls her mother an old hippie, and they all go out together.

The impetus to end her marriage, which Hannah had mentally deserted a year after she entered it, was a direct result of the women's movement. She started reading books by feminists and learned that she was not alone in her feeling of a lifeless routine involving the supermarket, clean ashtrays, and a man in the house who, when he wasn't intruding on her space, was nearly invisible. "It always seemed to me there were an awful lot of women who thought there's more to life than this. I was aware of how lazy I was. I sat there all those years scared to death to do anything with my talents. I was bored with my husband and I had no interest in sex with him. I spent most of the marriage working at better jobs to put him through school as a teacher, and helping him to get his master's degree. We settled into a marital cliché. I knew where all his socks were and the house had become a real bore. It took me three years to gather my forces until I could leave him. My mother finally settled it. She said she knew I was unhappy and she would support me if I got a divorce."

Before the marriage ended, Hannah's husband introduced her to Grant, who taught choral music at his school. Hannah was learning to play the guitar and, well, it's the same old story. Hannah started seeing Grant and eventually told her husband to leave. She confesses: "It was callous but I was never so happy to see anyone walk out the door. It all represented such a waste. I know it's not his fault. He's a perfectly fine person but it should never have happened. People are afraid to recognize that this is not a loving relationship. They're scared to be with someone else or to be alone."

Grant and Hannah talk in tandem, spelling each other off. They laugh at the same things but emotionally they're quite different. His heroes are tragic and romantic and throw themselves off bridges. He considers himself illogical. Hannah is practical and rational and her heroes are survivors. She is both frustrated and turned on by his sudden change of moods and wall-banging frustrations. She needs to be with someone who is unpredictable, who can teach her to be more spontaneous. Grant has learned to relax, trust what's going to happen, and believe that things will somehow be right.

Sexual fidelity is something they have never practiced. The truth, they say, is that people who haven't had an affair would if they could. This reminds me of a crusty divorce lawyer who told me curtly: "The only reason people stay together is because they can't find anybody else." They have a verbal contract which neither has violated as far as they know. Both are free to have sex with other people but they must tell the other about it. No hidden affairs. That kills relationships. Still, for a couple of years they remained faithful until some interesting people began drifting in and out of their lives, particularly through Hannah's work with an academic group studying human sexuality. One or the other would be late after work or they would agree to leave parties with other partners. After one party, they decided to take the experiment a little further. They invited another couple to share their king-sized bed and changed partners. Grant says now he didn't feel "very good" about it. Hannah found it exciting to watch Grant and the other woman. It's not an experience they are likely to repeat but they are prepared to see how "open" a relationship can be. The other woman involved stopped being Hannah's friend, and soon after she broke up with her husband. Hannah and Grant admit they had a hand in pushing an already floundering marriage over the brink. Hannah also admitted to being fiercely jealous of this woman because she might later try to see Grant alone. She was trying desperately to rationalize the feeling: "People invest too much in sex. It's not the sex, it's putting a romantic thing on it."

Hannah has several admirers who take her out and she has many sexual offers. Sometimes she does something about it. Working for a sex research center, she talks about sex all day and is constantly in the presence of men. She insists on knowing a potential sex partner well before having a relationship. She says what usually happens is they have a mild flirtation and become friends instead of lovers.

Grant is not at all cautious in his approach to women. "I wind up doing what I feel like doing at the moment and I usually pay through the nose. You get into so much trouble that I don't even try many times." So far, it has been a series of brief encounters for both of them. Hannah explains why: "You can get it on for fun but you cannot threaten the relationship. This is the unspoken fear." Grant wondered aloud why his one-night stands were often disasters. "In matters that pertain to sex, I wonder if I am making any progress, if I am growing at all. You manage better if you tend not to romanticize."

"That's obvious," Hannah explains. "Men are more romantically inclined. Women are able to do these things and enjoy them and let it go. Men won't let go even though they make all these jokes about casual sex and how women just won't leave them alone. In most cases, it's just the opposite."

Hannah seems to have more of a problem with jealousy even though Grant is the one-night-stand man and she sometimes toys with her partners for weeks and months before becoming sexually involved. She has never forgotten one party when Grant came to her and pointed out the woman he wanted to leave with. "I just waited at home for him in bed. What was uppermost in my mind, what I really wanted to know, was 'Does he still love me? Is he going to come home?'

It's wanting to know things are still the same. I think about whether someone else is going to be better than me." She doesn't like to admit it but she has actually said to Grant: "Have you found anybody who does that better than me?" The question humiliates her as a woman who is liberated and in charge of her own sexuality, but when she is in such a frame of mood they sit up and talk all night. There are tears and rages and a very tough evaluation of what is and is not acceptable in these outside excursions.

There aren't many men who tolerate women having affairs and maybe that includes him, Grant says. When I asked why he accepts Hannah's lovers, he doesn't so much answer as set out the problem they're trying to resolve. "I can't see any kind of system working where there is one set of rules for the woman and another for the man. I'm trying to work toward the view of a relationship we can both live with." Hannah concedes that their brave new venture doesn't mean it works or that they don't have problems. "But I'd rather have the agony of keeping it open and honest than go through a series of two- or three-year relationships for the rest of my life. It's the only thing that works for me."

Grant doubts he would have experienced so much personal growth if it hadn't been for his open relationship, but there are definite limits to growth, certain rigid rules about civility. As Hannah put it: "If Grant calls me out of the blue about seeing another woman, it freaks me out." He is aware of this. "It would be like her calling me and telling me half the house burned down and I couldn't come home. Sometimes I go to her office and talk to her if that's going to happen."

Hannah elaborates. "Part of the contract is that you don't throw that on somebody. You really try to see if it's comfortable with the other person. If it's not, then you have to talk it out some more." So far Hannah has never asked Grant to stop seeing someone when these circumstances arrive, but Grant warns her bluntly: "I'm still my own person. I'm willing to check it out. But when I have something else to do, it doesn't mean I don't love you. If you said no, I don't know how I would react. I might get angry." Hannah lets this glide by, supremely confident that Grant will carve some of the harshness out of this absolute statement. And he does. "Hannah has the absolute right to refuse if she feels the other woman is out to rip me off or if she is destructive and wants to catch me permanently."

On her part, Hannah knows Grant feels jealous when she is with men who have money or position and who might be able to lure her away. Basically, all their partners have been friends or at least known to both of them. There has been no sense of threatening competition. As Hannah explains: "If he gets it on with a close friend that would be fine, but it would be intolerable if it were a complete stranger."

Open marriages bewilder me in many ways, but I think I can take a measurement here. Graham and Irene have one-night stands out of town where they're not likely to run into the other people again. Hannah and Grant also seem to be one-night-stand people but they want to keep it friendly and in the family so they can take careful notice of what is going on. Close encounters with strangers seem to be taboo because Hannah and Grant both admit to a "fear of the unknown." Somebody just might turn out to be "better."

When they come home from their encounters, they arrive as equals and the other person is not supposed to be sitting there wringing his or her hands. They may be cool toward each other, they may have to talk it out, but an uncontrolled scene is not part of the contract. Hannah says she is a selfish person. With a hint of near-malice in her voice, she says there have only been two people she ever felt guilty about. "My mother and my grandmother. Never men!" Her sexual adventures have simply been a matter of reasserting her attractiveness. Or, as she sees it, finding out how she's doing in the world at large. Her experiences with other men have not been emotional but stroking for the good old ego. Not having other sexual encounters, Grant says, is like telling yourself you can run anytime you want to but you never go out and do it. Proving yourself attractive serves a purpose but Grant wonders if it is a validation of personal worth.

While Grant worries whether sexual attractiveness has anything to do with being a worthy person, Hannah announces: "God forbid, I may wake up in five years and want to be married and having kids. And I hope I understand these things while they're happening. I want to control my own destiny. I want to get what I want. My hope for women is that they know what they want and that they at least try." Back in the sixties when she was in the Haight-Ashbury she was smoking dope and she did the only thing you had to do then: be and let it be. "The difference now is to have real people talking about what they do and how they feel. I definitely agree with responsibility and commitment. This is what keeps me coming back to Grant."

Grant accepts this but it must be added that he will do anything to avoid the image, and the feeling that must accompany it, of being a settled-down couple. He wants to be able to look at himself when he's eighty-five years old and say he did what he felt like doing. Still, the biggest thing they did was to move out of their separate apartments into this house. The next thing you know they were calling it "our house" and Grant was taking out the garbage. They split the bills and have their own bank accounts, which is hardly radical these days. Hannah says if it's necessary to put some label on their relationship, say this: "We're quasi-monogamous street people."

I was walking down their long stairway to the street and my mind was worrying about the seeming contradiction of commitment *and* freedom beneath the sheets. With her personal experience and her professional study of human sexuality, I asked Hannah, rather wearily: "Is there anything new under the sun about sex?" Hannah replied: "Absolutely nothing." Precisely.

7

Boys and Girls Together
Homosexuals

There's no question I was nervous at first at the prospect of talking to two men about their lives together as homosexuals. Leonard and I warily appraised each other over a long coffee table of liqueurs which his lover, Marvin, kept replenishing. Breaking an awkward mood, Leonard stood up suddenly and said, "Come see my office, my canary, my dog, and my cat," and then he flung open the door of a room and I saw a large bed with an enormous headboard and he announced in a loud, beautifully dramatic voice: "The *nuptial* chamber!"

As I laughed and blushed, an image of a Philadelphia judge came back to me. I had told him I was including a chapter on homosexual couples in my book and he told me: "I hope you're not presenting them in any sympathetic light." I considered his prejudice and ignorance, and my own, and I thought how he might have bridled if he read the study on homosexuals brought out in 1978 by the Institute for Sex Research at Indiana University. Considered the most comprehensive look at the social and psychological adjustment of homosexuals, the authors concluded, after interviews with 979 gay men and women in the San Francisco Bay area, that many homosexuals are more like ordinary married heterosexuals than the unhappy, unstable and highly promiscuous people the stereotypers would have them be. The authors discovered five types of homosexuals, each with different behavior patterns.

The six gays I interviewed, four men and two women, belong to the study's "closed couples" category. I deliberately sought out homosexuals who had been living together a long time, who were considered settled and adjusted, and who were well regarded inside the homosexual circle and without. My reasoning was simple: while there are a million "flaming faggot" jokes, there are not too many reports on gays who are successfully striving for lives of dignity. Perhaps a gay contact in San Francisco expressed it better: "If you just want any gay couples, you can find them on the streets, but that would be a disservice. There are couples in our community we all look up to."

"Closed couples" are described as people living in quasi marriages characterized by self-acceptance, contentment, and a high degree of sexual fidelity. The relationships tended to be long-standing, to reflect a strong emotional commitment and a stable sharing of household responsibilities. As a group, the closed couples scored higher on a happiness scale than the heterosexuals. Until they established a closed-couple relationship, many gay males reported a very active sex life, comparable to the heterosexual swinger but, as lesbians had already told me, the study showed that gay women had very few sexual partners; the majority had stable relationships with one other woman. For the "queer" baiters, the study contends that heterosexuals are far more likely than homosexuals to seduce minors, or to make unwanted sexual advances.

The gay couples I met had been together more than twenty years. I saw in them the same endless struggle to bring two disparate human beings together in warmth, to understand their own possibly conflicting desires, and to learn to deal with compromise as a willing sacrifice to the larger goal of remaining with each other. In these essential matters, all couples are the same. Some achieve these goals; some don't.

Leonard and Marvin live a few minutes from the beach in Vancouver in a neat, compact house with a beautiful garden where they spend much of their time on good days working, writing, and entertaining. They are respected and liked by others in the gay community, especially by young people who see them as gurus. Leonard is a successful author with an unabashed appreciation of spirits, both gay and liquid. He has a big belly which he shows off in T-shirts, and his mobile face shows signs of full-tilt living. There is a mischief, a touch of decadence, and the awareness that he is always thinking over what you are saying. None of his talk seems idle, although it is frequently hilarious. He is obsessed with beautifully wrought words and carefully constructed thoughts which show in his writings and his conversations. He is capable of wildly shifting moods, petulance, and can be demanding of those about him.

Compared to Marvin, his lover of twenty-five years, Leonard is selfish. Marvin is tall and slim with a pouf of gray-and-white hair encircling his head, almost like the head of a dandelion in seed. He is a professor, soft-spoken and reserved, and, while he is expressive in his opinions, he does not over-assert or argue. He and Leonard are opposites, which has resulted in problems, but they complement each other, and both have made compromises that have kept them together.

I have to admit that the first time I arranged an interview with Leonard and Marvin over lunch at their house, I drank too much wine, laughed too much, and didn't take any notes. Marvin had made an excellent salmon quiche; he had poured the good white wine and, afterward, made Leonard's dry-as-dust martinis. I complimented Marvin on his cooking and felt strangely sexist in pointing to a male-female role in their relationship. Leonard quickly warned me not to make the ridiculous assumption that Marvin wore the apron and he wore the trousers.

During the days I knew Leonard and Marvin, and over the months and years I have known other couples, I realized that not everyone wants to escape everyday chores and roles. In particular, I found with long-lasting gay couples that there is no liberation struggle within the household. Leonard cleans and takes out the garbage, and Marvin cooks and serves drinks. This was determined long ago because that happened to be what they were good at. The domestic role-playing of heterosexual couples doesn't seem to be a major issue.

Leonard and Marvin, now in their fifties, met in Paris, where Leonard was about to become an Anglican priest, and had published a book on religious architecture. Marvin was twenty-one, rootless, and in an emotional crisis. Leonard believes he loved him at first sight. For him, it continues to be ironical that this young, confused student whom he had to protect, possibly forever, evolved into a respected teacher surrounded by students who merely nod in passing to Leonard, the published author, the worldly, experienced man. Marvin's growth and individuality so confound him that he throws up his hands and makes of their affection a physical analogy. "He's so much taller. I run around like a terrier after him."

There were years of separations in Europe and in the United States before Leonard and Marvin settled sixteen years ago in their house in Vancouver, a city large enough so that they could feel they wouldn't stand out. The frustrating struggle to find jobs in the same cities, they feel, has strengthened their union. Then the real problem began. The man Leonard had always thought of as a student was now a scholar with a following, and he seemed an entirely different person. Leonard, the sensitive creator of fictional characters, had possibly created an unreal character for Marvin. "I now had to accept Marvin as an involved human being. I had a measure of public acclaim with my books but suddenly he was meeting young people to whom he was *the* most important person. For me, the hardest thing was to accept Marvin in his own right with a world that was making claims on him. There wasn't just *me* anymore."

Now that they are older, they have found they have more in common with couples whether they're gay or not. Leonard says it's because all couples have the same problems: how they get along with each other's families; how they're perceived as individuals and as a couple; whether they're equal; how the extra money is spent; what they do about sexual indifference or infidelity; how they accept their partners' need to be alone.

They are pleased that they are still attractive to each other and to other people, and that they are in good health. They are sexually active and consider themselves lucky. They know, like the rest of us, that as they get older this too may pass away.

An abiding respect for individuality keeps the relationship running smoothly much of the time; at other times, the assertion of too much individuality, usually on Leonard's part, causes rifts. On any given day, Leonard is in the house writing, listening to every sound around him. He watches uneasy seasons out of his windows. He is emotionally responsive to a sudden leaf falling. He accepts no telephone calls; all is silence waiting for him. When Marvin comes home from teaching, Leonard wants his company and a noisy, salonlike atmosphere. Marvin has had meetings and classes all day; he wants a quiet dinner and an evening that drifts past in unspoken contentment. Sometimes, someone is bound to go to bed early and disappointed.

Still, as Leonard says, the most important thing is whose head is on the pillow beside you when you wake up. "The pattern of my life revolves around one other person," he says. "It's the choreography of my life that I like best. It's nice to have guests and then lie in bed and gossip about them." There have been some brief love affairs, men Leonard thought he loved, and there have been the orgies at the steambaths when he packed his old kit bag and told Marvin he would be back in about twenty-four hours—totally *exhausted*.

"All males are promiscuous," he explains. "Every heterosexual male tells me of the chicks he's laid. At a certain stage gay men are more promiscuous than heterosexuals. I used to go to the steambaths for sex, for choreographed promiscuity, but I was pressured, and I was hung over, and I didn't get my writing done. Now I'm much older and I don't have any interest in steambaths anymore." At this point, Marvin enters the conversation: "I didn't feel jealous when you went to the steambaths. It just meant that you weren't talking to me anymore. I don't think that I'm jealous or possessive about your different lives." Leonard remarks on how very long they've been together. "Remember the wedding cake?" he asks, roaring with laughter. (On their twenty-fifth anniversary some straight friends brought them an enormous cake with two little grooms on it.) They slip briefly into banalities, giving little signals of how pleased they are with each other, and in this they are not the least different from any other older couple. They have matured well together.

Leonard considers their relationship a "marriage," although he can't stand the sentimentality of the wedding vows. "As far as sexual infidelity is concerned," Marvin says, "this is a global problem. As long as it's not flaunted or habitual I don't see any problem. But I do think sometimes that one just goes too far."

The years together have been hard won by Leonard and Marvin. Leonard is given to exploring his nature, not without hurt to others. He does not believe that strictly observed monogamy would work for him but he appreciates its intrinsic value. Time has tempered his outside sexual interests but so has the hard, cold fact that he doesn't really like having his lover with someone else. He asks me: "Regardless of your loins, where does it stop? In the end it has to be the roof over you. That's awfully important."

As illustration, Leonard described a weekend he spent in New York as a guest of an aging American poet, and the sadness he felt for the poet when his lover arrived with his current male friend. It struck Leonard, though not for the first time, that he never wanted to be in the same situation, where he would have to scream at Marvin: *"Who* is this guy?" No person really handles jealousy well, he supposed.

In the time they've been together, Leonard has "fallen in love" twice—after their first decade, and then again six years ago. Leonard felt he had a right to these experiences but he also felt guilty. The moment Marvin told him to end his affairs, he did. Leonard says you have to guard against the powers of rationalization, that part of you that can find a reason for any kind of behavior. They came through the rough parts because they genuinely believed they were the best for each other. Leonard explains: "There are times at my age when I think I could be having far more sex than I do but you have to have a series of priorities. I'm not prepared to pay the price of sexual promiscuity. You can't legislate loyalty or monogamy but you can have a relationship with a degree of articulation that can stand the crisis of a minilove. It won't eliminate the pain but it's better than not existing. It's important to say to Marvin, 'I think I'm falling in love,' and to even get a laugh out of it. Romance thrives on secretiveness. That degree of candor can be useful in keeping an outside interest in proportion. After all, you *can* fall in love for twenty-four hours. That comes at certain times for men and women. In France, it's legitimate for women of thirty-nine to fall in love with a seventeen-year-old boy. In our society that woman would be reviled. We turn it into vaudeville jokes about the mailman or the delivery boy. Now women are sharing their days with men at the office, and there is going to be more and more of this. It's changing relationships."

Leonard believes a relationship has a better chance of surviving if you enter it assuming there will be sexual strains. It is destructive to overromanticize relationships, especially monogamous ones. He says if monogamy is a central value to your relationship, sex may become routine and ecstasy is likely to fly out the window. Monotony is sometimes the price you pay.

"We have created a superromantic concept of marriage when in fact it is a very bleak, cruel laboratory of human relationships. It is the struggle of coming together as equals. Love is a basic human appetite, as necessary as sleep and food, but if we make a relationship contingent upon men's erections going in loyal directions, let's forget marriage. You can't base a relationship on physical attraction. She gets wrinkles, you get dentures. Only a husband, not a lover, knows that a woman's hair gets thin as she ages, and if he loves her he never lets on. These are the everyday realities and they can sweeten aging if there has been a healthy relationship. When a woman of sixty says, 'I still love the old fart,' she's taking him dentures, baldness, and all. That's the richest thing on the planet.

You know, we're chucking off far too many values. Marriage remains what is best for most people. And there is a little thing like children. The prisons are full of people from broken marriages. I spend a lot of time worrying about tomorrow's children. I have godchildren of my own. I haven't left the human race because I'm gay."

Young people come regularly to Marvin and Leonard's home, and there has never been a jealous competition over them. Any promiscuity by either has been conducted far from their premises. Their gay parties can be academic and intellectual, bawdy and replete with limp-wristed parodies of themselves, but the unspoken rule is that the guests have commitments to other people. There are no dates made here. It is the same sense of trust that one respects at intimate parties given by heterosexual couples who are friends of long standing. A home is neither a steambath nor a trysting place.

Leonard says he is more generous than Marvin with his time with other people and tends to say yes to anyone who wants to come into their lives. Marvin admits to being the protector. He takes the telephone off the hook. He answers the calls and decides whether to disturb Leonard or take a message. Leonard says it is vital to know your role in a relationship and to have a sense of "idiocy," to be able to laugh at yourself. Marvin enlarges: "Leonard prefers to laugh at himself than to have people laugh at him. I think all fights in an old relationship are trivial. They're never about life and death and creativity. They're usually about why you didn't buy the celery at a certain supermarket." He makes a slight grimace, letting me know that he and Leonard survive the same domestic trivia as the rest of us.

Loving Marvin has given Leonard "enormous social insurance" and has made his life one thousand times easier, he says. "Love is not all romantic," Marvin explains. "It is having someone to help you get through life. It is *edifying* the other person."

Leonard recalls that he lived and made friends in Vancouver for a year before Marvin was able to join him. When

Marvin moved in, Leonard invited everyone he knew to meet his lover so they could see the situation for what it was. They have never made a secret of their homosexuality, and only one straight couple couldn't accept them. In academic circles, Leonard is treated as Marvin's partner and they are asked out as a couple. Vancouver is known as a tolerant city, and people seem to accept the person, not the stereotype.

They believe the success of a relationship demands learning how to combine oneness and separateness, or, as Leonard put it, underlining every word: "When I'm in my studio, I'm *in* there!" Being alone when you have to be is not measured by floor space but by the acceptance and understanding of the other person. Leonard suggests: "Half the relationships are on the rocks because they're in each other's hair. It's asphyxiation." Being opposite types, what pleases Leonard about Marvin is the way they have grown to know exactly what the other is going to say at any given moment, and how they will react. Predictability bores some people, but it is a triumph for others to have such intimate knowledge of how another person feels and—most of all—to be pleased with the findings. Almost every couple I talked to used the phrase "extrasensory perception" to describe how in tune they are. Some of them have made the same observation I have: Very old people who have lived in harmony seem toward the end of their lives to *physically* resemble each other.

Leonard says the reason so many people come to them for advice (young girls confide in them about their boyfriends and their love lives) is that they can see the success of their relationship despite its ups and downs. "I am not the world's greatest person to live with all the time," Leonard admits. "Marvin is ordered and practical and I can go on Cloud Nine and into incredible moods. Sometimes I'm not really here and it's almost necessary for him to type up a list of instructions for me, and I make a point of following them." In his mind, Marvin had almost become his secretary-housekeeper and it was a personal hurdle Leonard had to overcome. He was beginning to let him do too much for him. Marvin was cooking, he was writing the checks, and it even went beyond that. "I felt the next thing he'd be doing was cleaning my teeth. Then Marvin's life became busier and I realized there are limits to how irresponsible you can be."

Now no decisions are unilateral. They plan together the details of their dinner parties right down to where the name cards will be placed at the table. They need a new roof but they also want another dog, and that has to be worked out. "We're very civil to each other. I always say good morning to Marvin when he brings me my orange juice and vitamins and tea. I never forget to say thank you. I'm spoiled rotten and I'm aware that Marvin likes to do things for me. But it still behooves me to be appreciative. He has said 'I love you' only three times in our lives but he shows me every day."

Jeremy and Morris live in a Victorian house in San Francisco and for the past few years, their focus has been not on how to live as homosexual lovers in a heterosexual world but how much time they have left together. Jeremy developed congestive heart failure and it has brought a dramatic change to their life-style. Morris has been all too happy to adjust as best he can—that's the easy part—but to watch his lover become frail, to see him walk so slowly, to observe how he must deliberately take time for breathing, is something nobody can prepare for.

Morris is robust, exuding health, and at fifty-one he's three years older than Jeremy. There is a sorrow, an almost apologetic air about him, as he strides across a room while Jeremy sits there almost measuring the time until he has to go back to bed and rest. To suddenly become almost inactive has been a stunning blow to both of them. Their gentleness with each other and their affection is intense because it is moment to moment, not something they can let slide for a few days or weeks. They remind me of very old people who, when one becomes incapacitated, the other almost breathes for his partner, and hopes that if he can't get better, at least he won't get worse. What a lasting relationship means, in the end, to Jeremy, so emaciated, is having a partner who cares about the shadow of himself.

"When I was sick," Jeremy told me, not looking at Morris, "I was fearful of his reaction. I really felt there might be a rejection, and I could have understood it." Morris wants no more of this kind of talk: "We changed the way we do things because Jeremy doesn't have the stamina, but we still have the companionship. And what that means is you have someone you can be the best and the worst with and he won't walk out."

Jeremy and Morris are reticent with me and we begin by talking about the political climate for gays in San Francisco. Although things aren't as hateful as they were in the fifties when Morris and Jeremy got together, they still have hatemongering people to look out for, and periodic state bills demanding that male teachers prove they're not homosexual. But still this is a city of seven hundred thousand people where 25 per cent of the registered voters are estimated to be homosexual. It is a city of some 160 gay bars and the degree of political and social acceptance of gays is such that thousands of American and Canadian homosexuals have chosen to move here.

Jeremy and Morris have always worked for gay rights and human rights. Their names are often given to new arrivals in the city by gay contacts because they are well known as a long-lasting, committed couple serious about doing something for the whole community, not just for gays. We first talked about their uphill political struggle, and then moved on to their histories.

Both Jeremy and Morris had been married to women. They met at a difficult time when they were preparing for divorces. Morris had been married for twelve years and the marriage seemed all right to him but nothing was ever first-rate. He considered himself an average married man but gradually had to take note of his homosexual tendencies and urges. Accepting them took years of inner turmoil and he went into counseling with his wife. He was tormented about what was the moral thing to do, whether he should break up a "reasonable marriage." Morris had no children, nor did Jeremy from his four-year marriage.

Jeremy always knew he was gay and it wasn't hard for others to guess, even when he was a young boy. He had brief gay encounters before he was married, but because he was raised in a strict religion, he always felt wrong about what he was doing and thinking. After a painful break with a male lover, and losing his job because he was discovered to be homosexual, he met a girl he converted to his own religion. He told her he was gay and she told him she could change him. He thought that with faith and a "normal" kind of love, he might find some kind of peace.

Jeremy described his marriage as "pretty good," but there is an unreality when he speaks of it. Jeremy sees religion as bringing him and his wife together and taking them apart. As she became more involved in the church, he became more and more doubting, and was excommunicated when he was exposed as a homosexual. His wife's doing, he suspects. Morris and Jeremy met through mutual friends on the third Saturday in October 1959. Morris was in private practice as a lawyer and was renting a room from a gay friend who was not his lover. Jeremy was a hospital technician and he, too, was living platonically with a man. Within three months, they had their own apartment together.

The marriage vow is a promise to stay together forever and it is a tattered remnant for many, but I have yet to meet anyone who married with the intention of getting divorced. The tendency is to be married as long as it lasts. And the dream is to last. The comparison of the marriage vow and the agreements made for a long-term relationship between homosexuals is odious to many heterosexuals because, after all, two men or two women living together and sexually loving each other is morally unacceptable to a majority of our society. But fidelity is a common root in almost all couplings. Many of us don't live up to the ideal of fidelity; we either initiate infidelity or go along with it. Still, if some sort of loyalty to our partners survives and we stay together in spite of the hurt, if we survive the opposing desires to both approach and depart from our partners, it becomes a *symbiotic* resting place. Jeremy and Morris are an example of this theory in practice.

Jeremy calls their situation "habitual." There were no specific rules when they set out and there have been stages when they were less than monogamous, but Jeremy says they always had the *intention* of loyalty. "It's okay," Jeremy says, "if one of us is in Europe and something happens, but if Morris is home I wouldn't go to the steambaths or the bars. We have cast our lot together and that means a commitment, even though it can sometimes be counter to our desires."

Most homosexuals debate the use of the word "marriage" to describe long-term relationships between gays. The lament is that although marriage nearly exactly describes their life-style, marriage still is an exclusively heterosexual institution. Although I found in my research that some lesbians wanted to be seen within the context of marriage, they suggested that this was part of their female upbringing. Morris hates the concept of marriage because he considers it archaic. Society evolved marriage, he insists, to keep people prisoners, which is precisely what many feminists have been saying all along. Morris says it is far better to have some sort of arrangement with no name and no legal contract.

When people marry, Morris says, they make demands they wouldn't otherwise, and he's pleased that more young couples are choosing to live together without a document. He doesn't think it connotes promiscuity; it may mean they're secure enough in their affection that they don't need the force of a law as some security against abandonment. Nevertheless, he admits that he has known some "marvelous" marriages, and that for some people the formal institution is meaningful and essential for personal fulfillment.

Just as with married heterosexual couples, Morris says there is no consensus among gay people about joint bank accounts and the sharing of assets. They have the same bitterness about their possessions when they split that heterosexuals have when they divorce. Morris has acted as lawyer on some of these cases and nothing seems more pitiful to him than two gays fighting over the china. Jeremy and Morris choose to be communal about their property and neither feels that any particular item in their home belongs to one or the other exclusively. Their money also flows between them. Morris says: "We're economically independent and we don't give a shit if we're accepted."

Until Jeremy's illness, they regularly traveled to Europe, attended the opera and symphony, and dined out. They are both active in their respective churches, which they are quick to point out are not gay churches. They go to the coffee hours and the potluck suppers and know most of the parishioners at both their churches. When a couple has a religion, Morris says, it gives stability to their lives. Jeremy says: "The sacraments are very important to me. They add a sustaining dimension."

Something else that sustains them is that they have come to terms with the romantic trap of love. Many relationships fail because people believe that romance is the answer to everything, that it really is possible to live happily ever after. Everyone knows misery and quiet desperation from time to time, and that's when it is critical to be able to share and understand and, also, to be able to step aside and let the other partner come to grips with his private griefs.

Jeremy, his frail hands resting in his lap, smiles. He has fully considered his physical condition. "It's nice," he says, "when you can laugh with each other as you hit middle age and you get fat and you get a pot belly." Because they are the same sex and can empathize with what the other is going through, Morris and Jeremy feel they've avoided much of the psychological alarm that the midlife period causes for so many men and women. They particularly sympathize with older women who have concentrated on their homes and children, and are left absolutely empty. Perhaps it's not as bad now, they say, as more women develop careers.

When couples stay together they collect memories, but the

longer their relationship lasts, the less memories consist of great, exciting moments. They become warm, small things that would not be of consequence to anyone else. Morris told me about the time he opened his law office and Jeremy came by to lay carpeting, and then they had supper afterward. It was a quiet, loving evening; one of the finest memories he has.

To survive, it is necessary to concentrate on those interests you have in common. Jeremy and Morris love music and reading and they talk over what they have heard and read. Before Jeremy's illness, they had a ritual of getting up early in the morning, making the coffee, and squeezing the orange juice. Then, as now, they spend an hour or more talking about the food-importing business they started a few years ago, and they read the newspapers together, gossiping over the items.

Morris has never thought of leaving Jeremy over these past twenty years, but Jeremy almost walked out after he learned he was sick. Jeremy's doctor told him at first his need to change was a symptom of shock combined with the midlife crisis; all his problems were psychosomatic. But Jeremy finally became obsessed with the idea of breaking up and said so to Morris, who told him: "If it makes you happy, we can live apart." Jeremy looked at him and asked, "Do you want to?" and when Morris replied, "No, it's unthinkable," Jeremy knew he had a companion for life.

Before they met, Clare and Adele lived lives of subterfuge and guilt and spent a lot of time in progressive libraries reading books on what they, as lesbians, were supposed to be and feel. From denial of their sexual inclinations, they went on to become pioneers in the lesbian, gay, and women's movements in San Francisco. They're city officials and with great pride they showed me the scroll they received from the city government on the occasion of their twenty-fifth "wedding" anniversary. The scroll commemorated their "being together." Over two days five hundred friends and notables dropped by their house to congratulate them.

In their early years Clare acted as the "butch" and Adele was the "femme," terms used for the male and female sides of a lesbian couple. When I met them, they fit the physical stereotype, Clare with her cropped gray hair and square, mannish build and her cigars. She had a belligerent, suspicious air about being interviewed by an unknown straight. Adele had talked her into it. She is slighter, smiling, hostessy, as she brings out the cheese and martinis. In a book they co-authored, *Lesbian/Woman,* published in 1972, they described how they accepted their roles as butch and femme and to outward appearances they have stuck with them, no matter how womanly they both are. They wrote: "The only model we knew, a pattern that also seemed to hold true for those few lesbians we had met, was that of mom-and-dad or heterosexual marriage. So Clare assumed the role of butch (she was working at the time) and Adele, being completely brainwashed in society's role of women anyway, decided she must be the femme. Like her mother before her, she got up every morning to make breakfast—at least for the first week." Lesbians in their age groups did this all the time, but over the years they got out of the trap and decided they were women, period.

Sitting in their old house on top of a slope where a large picture window invites you to stare at downtown San Francisco lights, I found myself uneasily sipping my drink. I had established easy rapport with male homosexuals. We laughed, we made fun of their stereotypes, and I loved it after a gay party when all the men kissed each other wetly on the lips and placed a discreet cheek against mine. But the first thing I had to face with Adele and Clare was, simply, that they were of my sex and their loving disclosures were going to have more direct impact on me than anything two male lovers told me. Clare might have been reading my thoughts: "We're organized politically and we are recognized as a voting bloc, but we have no illusion that people love us." Adele told me: "If you're really secure about your own sexuality, you don't worry about someone else's."

These women told me that lesbianism doesn't just happen. You don't wake up one morning and say "I am one" or "This is how I'm going to be from now on." As a child, Clare never related to boys and while she played tag with all the kids in the neighborhood, she loved to play "house" with the girls and be the "daddy." That meant being the boss and laying down the rules. But the games children play don't last long enough to take on meaning, and Clare found herself a teenager listening endlessly to girls talking about boys. She had some doubts stirring but she went *their* way and married at nineteen when she was in her third year of college.

Clare and her husband both worked on the college paper and shared interests. When they married, she was relieved to know that she was really in love with a man. They had a daughter and her husband's job kept him on the road. What she began to feel has become the cliché of women of the last decade. Trapped. No identity. A wife and mother and nothing else. Her husband wanted a wife; the big difference in this scenario is that Clare wanted a wife too. Some trapped women have affairs, take university courses, go to work, or walk out. Clare fell in love with the next-door housewife. The housewife never found out, but Clare wrote some passionate letters she kept in the house and her husband discovered them. They tried to work things out for a while but divorce was inevitable.

Clare knew by then she was a lesbian and she wanted to be one. She thought about suicide, which is not uncommon for young lesbians, or for any people who are seriously different in "normal" society. Recognizing her own problems as a wife and as a mother, she gave custody of her daughter to her former husband.

Adele scarcely knew the word homosexual when she was a teenager. She dated boys, she liked to tease almost in the manner of a southern belle. She became engaged and backed out because of some certainty that marriage wasn't a future. And there was always a kind of disgust when a girlfriend would telephone and cancel a movie with her because some guy had made a date at the last minute. It seemed she had better times with girls than with boys.

Neither woman had had a lesbian affair at this stage and they went through years of feeling like outcasts, although they were sure there had to be other women out there who felt the same way they did. Meeting women who were their own kind was virtually impossible. Clare and Adele did meet in 1949, but for nearly four years they were just friends because Adele wasn't convinced she wasn't straight and dated men. They remember one night when they were working for a trade journal in Seattle and they were drinking at the press club. The subject came around to homosexuality. Clare announced: "Well, I'm one." Adele felt naïve and fascinated. "After Clare said she was a lesbian, I was afraid to get involved because I thought this kind of affair would follow the same pattern as the affairs I had with men. I never felt very pleased after I had won a man and I didn't want to screw up the friendship I was developing with Clare. So I managed to fend her off although I was dying to go to bed with her." But finally one day "Clare made a pass and I completed it." That first step was difficult because as Clare says: "It was taboo to make a move against a heterosexual woman or to bring her out. As far as I was concerned Adele was a heterosexual." Adele's first response was to run away, but after some emotional sorting out, they moved into an apartment together.

As soon as they were living together, Clare did something that was symbolic and psychologically important to her. She took Adele to the bank to open joint checking and savings accounts. Throughout her childhood, she had witnessed her father dole out her mother's allowance, and she vowed the same thing would never happen in her life. Financial arrangements had never been discussed, but Clare decided that they had entered a "marriage" and that meant mutual ownership of all assets. In essence, Adele says, that trip to the bank was "our marriage ceremony." Many lesbians do not pool their resources and conduct their financial affairs just as heterosexual roommates do. They split the food money and the rent money; one buys her stereo and the other buys her couch. After all, roommates presumably only stay together until something else comes along. Clare and Adele had agreed to only one thing—that they would stick it out for one year—but Clare's determined financial and household arrangements were an aggressive indication that she expected a whole lot more. "This sort of arrangement where everything is separate implies a built-in failure of a relationship, a sort of self-fulfilling prophecy. We weren't taking any chances."

The first difficult situation they had to resolve was Clare's daughter. In those days they pretended to be just friends living together, and they spent all their emotional energy maintaining the masquerade. Pressures built when Clare's daughter visited for the summer of their "honeymoon" and to make matters even worse, Adele continued to see a persistent boyfriend she was afraid to be truthful with. They were both invited to their respective families' homes for Christmas and holidays, and they successfully passed muster, but the deceit and the desire to declare their true relationship finally wore them down.

When Clare and Adele told their sisters and sent them books on lesbianism, they had no particular difficulty coping, but their parents spent years of pain and bewilderment before they finally came to accept them for what they are. Telling Clare's daughter the news was a different problem even though she visited her mother and Adele throughout adolescence and thought they had an admirable relationship, in fact just the kind of friendship she would like to have if she never met the right man. Clare was consumed by the idea of rejection when her daughter learned she was a lesbian. The subject was touched on one night when the girl was having dinner with them. She asked why they spent so much time with a women's club they belonged to—it was the earliest international organization for lesbians.

The next evening, Clare and her daughter were alone and she explained the aims of the organization. Her daughter still asked: "But why are you and Adele so involved?" Clare was taken aback. Had her daughter taken in nothing all those times she had seen male and female gays coming and going in the house? And she had been to gay social gatherings. No, it was apparently a surprise, so Clare carefully, and at length, explained the situation. There was no shock, no condemnation; instead Clare's daughter commented that it might be sort of interesting having two mothers instead of one.

Many lesbians come together with the idea of being monogamous, and Clare and Adele have been just that for twenty-five years, even though there has been jealousy, notably when Adele was still going out with her old boyfriend; then Clare put her foot down and made an issue of it, and that was that. There have been career jealousies as they moved into high-profile civic positions. Both having been journalists, the book they wrote together on lesbianism could not have been without professional rancor, but Clare must have won because it is her strong voice that echoes through the majority of the pages. Adele says: "People ask us if we fight. Hell, yes, all the time. If you have two people—two women, two men, or a man and a woman—and they say they never fight, that relationship will never last. But there is a difference in our fighting. You argue and you snarl over a specific issue but you keep it confined to that one thing. That argument is never allowed to spill over into any other aspects of our relationship."

The important thing I learned from Adele and Clare is that lesbians seek the same things anyone looks for in a lasting relationship: companionship, loyalty, shared interests, and the promise of a safe passage together when the unquestioned thrill of new love dissolves into the routine of closeness and responsibility. The advice Clare and Adele give to lesbians is fitting for all of us: Know yourself, accept who and what you are, and then take charge of your own destiny.

回顾

ロ repeated decorative border

8

The Gauguin Syndrome
Second Careers

In some relationships, particularly with men entering their forties, what can be called the Gauguin Syndrome takes over. The men affected by this have usually been absorbed in a career for fifteen or twenty years and generally they have been successful. But always at the back of their minds are cherished boyhood dreams that were shoved aside because they grew up in a time when every aspect of their lives was dictated by the expectations of their parents and society. Later, wives and children kept them locked into their responsibilities. The day they took on the huge life insurance policy, the child within supposedly died and the immature dreams were buried with them.

But for some men and women the creative force, the freer person, still lives and becomes more of a crisis in midlife than sexual longing or wandering. Unlike sex, which can be immediately gratified, this other desire gnaws on, and the fear is that it will never be satisfied. There are two ways of looking at these people who, at a certain stage in life, have an intense resurgence in the belief that they could still be the artist, poet, or writer, or a completely different and creative being, if there's enough time left. Some of them have a hope, but most of them have dust.

I think of the unrealistic Gauguins I know. People whose only life experience has been with the city who are suddenly beset with fantasies to return to the land they never set foot on. I think of the woman who forever talks of how she might have been an artist or a concert violinist if somebody had discovered her, if her sisters hadn't left her at home to take care of their mother. She has worked out in her mind the exact details of the night she might have played at Carnegie Hall, right down to the bouquet of yellow roses that would be thrown onto the stage. This is the kind of wistfulness most of us outgrow when we finally accept the fact that only enormous determination and talent might have brought us to within window-gazing distance of our dreams.

The most frustrated Gauguin people are those who successfully conduct an outer life and work part time, more or less secretly, at being artists and writers and nature people. They never know for sure if they're any good at it. Habit and circumstances hold most of them in pattern, but some break out and go the distance—for better or for worse.

I think of two friends who are intermediates in the Gauguin stakes and who might surprise everybody and do what they've been dreaming aloud so long. A male friend can identify trees and flowers and snakes, and has an ex-hippie son who actually went back to the land. The son has built a cabin and is making everything work by hand. Meanwhile, his father labors in a government office beset by memos and thoughts of woodpiles and whistles whittled from willow. His wife, always a city person, is engrossed in her work as a visiting nurse. He takes her on more frequent forays into the country on weekends, and every six months or so he tells me: "I think she's getting a little more used to the idea." A woman friend who describes herself as a housewife and volunteer worker has journals full of promising short stories, and complains bitterly sometimes of all the media people she knows who haven't helped publish her. When it is suggested that she see an agent or a publisher, she replies: "I'm not showing my intimate thoughts to some stranger." Maybe someday she, too, will get "used to the idea" and take her own first step.

Perhaps a few of us will be midlife geniuses; some of us will be midlife delinquents. Most of us, without renouncing the idea that all lives have space for dreams and spontaneity, can calmly acknowledge that fantasies usually are lovely—and gone. A psychiatrist told me we create an idealized image of ourselves as very young children, a time when we have all the dreams and none of the knowledge. As knowledge is acquired, the child's clear innocent vision recedes. He says if we have matured well, we accept this youthful time of dreaming for what it was, a stage. Some people, mature or otherwise, don't.

Dreams intruded into the lives of two couples I came to know for this book. The husbands have followed prescribed paths most of their lives. Now they are striking off in different directions to meet the hopes they had for themselves in their youth. I am certain one couple will confront the dream, and succeed or fail without damage to their relationship. The wife, in this case, has waited and pushed for her husband's dream as long as he has, and has opened some new ones for herself. I have my fingers crossed for the other couple. While it was easy to walk out of his office with his briefcase in hand, this man left some of his self-esteem behind. It's a crisis he has to resolve if he's ever going to be a Gauguin.

Basic to the stories of both couples in this chapter is that everybody did what they were expected to do most of their lives. The women followed the traditional values of staying home and raising children. Then in midlife they returned to universities to complete degrees, and are very successful at what they do. One man has written novels after hours and is going to do something about them. The other man has the walls of his house covered with fine sketches executed during stolen hours from a career at which he became very successful. They have no sex problems and no kid problems. One couple has no financial burdens; the other is always being given secondhand appliances and rugs from the family, but they certainly don't go garret-artist hungry. Both wives believe in their husbands' ambitions and will do a great deal to help accomplish them. They are not self-sacrificing, but neither are they like a woman I know who told her author-dreaming husband: "I'm going back to a job I hate so I can give you time off to write your book." Six months after scribbling notes in his daily journal, he took a high-paying commercial job and she said, somewhat cruelly: "What the hell was accomplished by that gesture?"

I went by bus to visit Angela and Theo, who live outside New York City. As with many people in this book, I had reached them through friends of friends and Theo bluntly told me: "Since you know good friends of mine, I would be delighted to entertain you. But that doesn't mean I'm going to *talk* to you. I'm private." I shoved my notebook down to the bottom of my carryall, which contained my usual gift bottle of a modest white wine, and held out little hope. The bus abandoned me on a stretch of highway near an ugly little motel in a field, and seeing no one to meet me I started to swear. Just then Angela and Theo pulled up in a station wagon, apologized for the bleak industrial landscape I had endured, and promised me I was going to a far better place. Minutes off the highway, we were sitting on a deck overlooking a small lake and eating clams. I couldn't believe such silence was possible only a short distance from New York. We talked about loons (the lake kind) and their children and my child; then we went inside the house for one of Angela's gourmet dinners, the kind they have almost every night of the week. I guess I was turning out all right, because Theo asked me when I was going to start taking notes.

Theo and Angela are forty-six and both are very trim and youthful looking. She is more open and sociable. His silences and dark-rimmed glasses make him appear more austere than he is. Theo, an optometrist, is precise about his wines and the carving of the meat and for a while, in the polite, almost fatherly atmosphere, I felt like one of his children's older friends. They have two daughters and a son and for one glorious year not long ago, they actually had the house to them-

selves. Now two children have moved back in and are further-
ing their education.

Angela doesn't cook for the children or do their laundry
and their presence doesn't bother the parents economically or
any other way. Their son, the aspiring musician, needs a few
more years to "expand." He knows nothing of the pressing
realities of his parents, who had to become educated and sala-
ried as soon as possible. Theo explains: "We had another kind
of freedom that comes with working hard and achieving goals.
Now some kids seem to need time to flounder around. The let-
it-all-hang-out philosophy of the sixties caused some ups and
downs for kids. But we never had great worries about aliena-
tion. There was some rebellion. It kept us on our toes, I suppose."

They were born and raised in the same small community
and married while they were in college. Angela dropped out
and worked as a secretary while he finished his studies. "Then
the three kids came along, the result of our unbridled passion,"
Theo jokes. For the first of several times, Angela warns that
her husband "kids a lot." Their parents provided them with an
apartment, and other financial help. There was never a time
when they felt overwhelmed by money problems. They managed to have wine or a drink in the house, but the cheapest
kind. Neither felt the necessity to plot their lives. For instance,
they never actually sat down and discussed if they wanted children or how many. They were so young, Theo says, that he
can't remember how he *felt* in those early days. Angela has
known this one thing all along: "I felt I truly loved this person
and it was the logical step to take. This was the early fifties
and there were no open relationships and no options. My feelings were very strong that I wanted to make a commitment.
On the other hand, my oldest daughter hasn't married and
doesn't want to. She feels very liberated."

Had there been other life-styles acceptable to the society
of his day, Theo concedes he probably would have tried them.
But monogamous marriage was the goal. He mentions his son,

who has lived periodically with his girlfriend, and says he neither approves nor disapproves. Moral values were taught a
long time ago and his children now are, simply, what they are.
There are no regrets in this area and, fortunately, there was no
grief with drugs, or unwanted babies, or hitting the road.
Their children are friendly and seem well adjusted, and they
get along well with their parents and their grandparents. Perhaps the children don't adhere to their traditional philosophy,
but they respect it.

Just as they came through their children's adolescence
without too much pain, Angela and Theo have managed to
remain faithful to each other for twenty-seven years without
feeling they have missed out on anything. Theo is introspective about his personal development, but he says he has never
minutely examined his marriage. I told him of a few people I
know who seem to be always looking at how they're doing together, as if there were a definable goal. For Theo, relationships *exist*. He says: "You can talk anything to death. And
it can be very harmful."

He views himself and his close male friends as contented
people who do not have a problem with sexual fidelity. "Sure,
some men and women are natural pursuers," he admits. "I
look at women, of course, but I also look at all the couples
with the money and the opportunity who don't fool around.
It's not that we have a lot of boring friends who are afraid to
do anything. I just think the inevitable crisis of sexual infidelity, particularly during the so-called male menopause, is
a stereotype that's been around too long." To be unfaithful can
be seen as a failure in moral character, Theo points out, but
monogamy is sometimes nothing more than the end product of
boredom and inertia. These are the couples who don't think
about their marriage, let alone something called monogamy.
Their concerns are the kids, their jobs, and their cars. There is
no fighting, no intimacy beyond sex. He believes there is such
a thing as a partnership that exists simply for the sake of
existing.

If there were ever an affair, Theo and Angela believe the other person should never be told or allowed to find out. Angela says she would not want to know. Theo believes it's sadistic to confess infidelity. "Tell your shrink instead," he says. "Why tell the person who you have hurt so much? You have already done violence to the trust you have shared, so why compound it? One of the complications of affairs, which is too horrendous for me to contemplate, is the idea of splitting up and starting over. To have to go through another 'courtship' terrifies me. Let's face it, the average guy is a little chicken. He's a worker and a dreamer. He's not a scorer." He believes the more common reasons for relationships going on the rocks are in-laws, money, arguing over children, and intellectual incompatibility.

It wasn't until late in the evening that Angela turned to Theo and suggested that he talk about his writing because very soon he's going to follow that dream—and it's going to change their lives.

For three years, Theo has been winding down his optometry practice. Angela has been working in the office with him, and they go home every day for two-hour lunches. They often take three- and four-day weekends. Angela says Theo always wanted to be a writer, but that was hardly considered a career in their day. Maybe he had what it took to develop into a writer, but the reality was that he knew he'd be a very good optometrist. He has completed several novels but he has stayed in optometry so long because it's in his nature to finish things. Just as he has "finished" his family in the sense of any major developmental role he might play, he has now finished the business part of his life. It is time to go for it. There were even physical and emotional events that seemed to make it imperative that he get out. He mentions daylight robberies in his office, and the fact that clients with whom he once had rapport were seeming to become irritable and irritating. And perhaps that was his fault because of his increasing preoccupation with his writing.

Angela has prepared for this midlife change and is excited about getting started. She went back to university seven years ago and earned a degree in art history. She thinks about teaching or working in a museum. She also likes the idea of expanding the bookstore she and Theo established for their eldest daughter. Angela never had ambitions for herself before, and she supposes she should have. Theo has thought so. "I always wished you had more drive," he tells her. "I have had far too much of your time and attention. But then I think of how she was going to marry this football player who owns a liquor store. She would probably be working nights behind his counter. Now I don't feel so guilty."

Having enough money and a wife who is eager and supportive of a new venture doesn't take the crisis out of a career change. Theo is plain scared. Several years ago, Angela offered to work full time so he could have a year off to write. But he couldn't do it. At this point, he realizes he has to stop talking and typing away in some psychic basement.

Ralph Ellison (author of *The Invisible Man*) once saw some of his writing and liked it. That high praise aside, Theo knows he is no writer until he proves it to himself. He has regrets about not seriously trying years ago. He is ashamed at the number of times he put aside his works in progress. He made money instead and abandoned his childhood wish. Now Angela, his fortuitous circumstances, and an urge that must finally be contended with are forcing him to try for it—win or lose.

Theo says: "I worry that I am too conventional. I worry that if I start a new life-style I'll create new neuroses. I don't know how flexible I am. I have been an optometrist all my life and this is a very comforting and conservative position. Will I be able to handle a free, unconventional life?"

Janine and Gordon have a somewhat unconventional life but Gordon is not really happy because of the guilt pervading the artist he wants to be. As an engineer, he has owned his own company and worked for large firms in two Canadian provinces. But almost every time he has been promoted to a top position, he has dropped out and gone home to be a painter for a while. Janine feels he is too sensitive to be in the world of big business, even though that thought doesn't always comfort her when she surveys her hand-me-down rugs.

Gordon confesses that as soon as he learns the operation of a firm and starts moving up in the ranks, he can't take the hypocrisy anymore. Hypocrisy for him is the phoniness of a way of life he was forced into as a naïve kid under enormous family pressure to make his mark within a narrow range of approved professions. Success has often been within reach but he has been the happiest and the freest sitting on the beach, in a community outside Vancouver where he lives, listening to the gulls and sketching. For a time these intense interludes still the voice telling him he must have a career, and he must make enough money to give his family the better life.

Freeing the artist within has meant never staying in a position longer than three years, and often enough being financially supported by Janine. She is frustrated and sometimes angry, but she does understand in her own way why Gordon is like this. He is torn between his duty to make money and have status in the community, and wanting to be a serious, full-time artist, which, at forty-six years of age, he thinks is almost foolish to consider. At times the conflict between the necessity and the desire has been so cruel that he has half seriously told Janine she should leave him for someone who enjoys and understands the power of money.

It didn't take Janine many years to realize that big money would never come through Gordon, so she borrowed a sum from a relative, studied day and night for a university degree, and is now a school counselor. She loves the work and the people, the involvement with many other lives, and the sociability. Home is the quiet leveler, a time for introspection or a conversation with her husband about whether their lives and minds are continuing to touch. They don't have the money to entertain or to go out, except for the occasional movie or sandwich. The closeness they have achieved with so much time alone together has been fine. But, God! sometimes she wants so desperately to throw all caution away and go to a very expensive restaurant, or have a catered party for some of the interesting people they know but can't afford to entertain. There is no chance to indulge a whim; but that's a small and trivial thing, she thinks, an exchange of immediate gratification and material comfort for the knowledge that she is Gordon's soul mate and sole confidante.

The hope that someday her husband will be a good artist is imposed upon their two teenaged children, who have part-time jobs and have never received an allowance. Gordon's dream has become the entire family's dream; whether it's selfish or hopeless or both is something he will eventually have to resolve. This is inherent in the structure of the family. Everyone has come to understand that some years there is money, which may mean a vacation and something new for the house. Other times their pleasures consist of the free things that a tightly knit family provides for itself. Janine feels the children are probably stronger and more self-reliant because of their life-style. But she also knows that it is never easy for adolescents to accept that, unlike some of their friends, they can't have everything they want. When she is in a personal stock-taking mood, Janine realizes that if Gordon were the type of man who provided her with all the necessities and luxuries, she might not have been motivated to find her own interests and career. In their particular situation, she thinks things have a way of balancing out.

I talked to Gordon and Janine together and separately, and they are very forthright and similar in their respectful appraisal of each other. Gordon, a pleasant, bearded man who speaks softly and is almost too self-effacing, seemed contradictory and a little beyond understanding at times. Even Janine confesses she doesn't always know what is going on inside him. He has proven that he can be strong, dynamic, and successful as an engineer. Yet at the same time that he is explaining that only painting sustains him spiritually and emotionally, he will leave this work aside for weeks and weeks, and do nothing but housework. Sometimes he's waiting for the ideas to come; sometimes he doesn't believe in his portrait of the artist as a mature man. This is when Janine's heart sinks: "I really love him," she says, "but I hate it when I see him put on an apron for an indefinite length of time."

Constantly, in our conversations, a note of apology would creep into Gordon's voice for the way of life he has imposed on his family. He insists some of his colleagues probably don't respect him, but some personal friends of his described him as being "brave and gutsy" for trying to find what he wanted to be, instead of trading on his obviously marketable skills. Gordon wondered how many men have been as "lean" in productivity as he.

Janine has been supporting the family for nearly a year and Gordon feels that he has been getting a very strong message from her to settle on some work. She worries about his being in the house all the time, keeping in touch with the outside only by telephone. This is the kind of thinking consistent with his going back into the world of engineering. As an artist, shouldn't he be alone? How different and clearer it was eighteen years ago when they married.

Gordon then was not only traditional but, well, obedient. Following the example of other family members on the prairies, he told Janine to quit university because he did not want her involved with anything outside the home. Money and living well were the important goals, and along with joining the local clubs, he even took Arthur Murray dance lessons because it was the popular thing to do. He followed the rules and the social customs and he thought he was building the proper life for them both.

Janine has another point of view. "He was extremely chauvinistic," she told me. "In those days we'd have company and he'd say, 'You serve the drinks. That's what a hostess does.' He sat in the house like a guest and when the company left, he rolled up his socks and threw them in a corner for me to pick up. He wanted babies right away. I didn't, but I had them. I married at twenty and it was really a fight for my independence. I wanted to get away from my people. I went from one dependent situation to another. I was brought up this way." She didn't realize how many years it would take to become a different kind of person she could still live with.

In the beginning, in the tight community where everyone lived under the scrutiny of family and friends, they believed they should have everything their friends had, and preferably more. It never seemed to work out. As friends prospered and bought houses and cars, they couldn't keep up. When she was six months pregnant with her son, Gordon was struggling to put together an engineering business. Janine watched with no little jealousy as her girlfriends trotted around on exotic vacations. It was such a struggle to survive, and there was envy and guilt about not meeting the standards of their social set. An independent turn of mind and life-styles were not appreciated. Still, there was this nub of humor and rebellion which allowed them to have their private good times as they struggled to make ends meet. But until they had the nerve to break away from their town and move to British Columbia eleven years ago, they were the stereotypical young couple living under the thumb of two very domineering families. Janine's mother was an intrusion in particular.

Her mother kept telling Gordon he was a "good boy," that he had to be a joiner and he had to succeed. Both he and Janine took the easy way out by trying to perform to everyone's expectations. Gordon will make it, the families were saying, but all Gordon could see was that he was failing to establish a proper business and that a cleaning lady and trips were out. They stuck out the first years of marriage in their hometown under the alternating opprobrium and encouragement of family and friends.

When Gordon's business wasn't going well, Janine managed to get work with the government dispensing mothers' allowance checks and counseling deserted wives. That started to give her a different outlook on life. She dealt with the immediate poverty of other people's lives, and another kind of poverty in her own. They were clearly failing to live up to standards imposed on them, but couldn't they live up to some standards of their own making? She had learned in seven years of maturity and marriage certain things basic to herself. Wasn't it time to act on them?

Janine had figured out her parents. She grew up with the idea that they were the happiest couple she knew, but she learned later that they weren't. Her mother nagged and set the tone and standards of the household. Her father treated Janine as a princess and indulged her shamelessly, perhaps in compensation, perhaps in retaliation against her mother. But in front of company, they always presented a united stand. As a child, hadn't she always seen them work one against the other? It was a façade, perhaps a slight and necessary façade, but Janine felt deeply that her life with her husband had to be more honest than that.

There had always been a streak of rebelliousness in her, and a certain flouting of standards that was shocking at the time. She was a university student when she met Gordon, and she remembers the day he dropped his fraternity pin in her hand. She didn't want it because it was tantamount to being engaged. She told him she wasn't ready for marriage, but she would love to sleep with him—she was just a little ahead of her time. Gordon replied it was marriage or nothing. She relented because she was afraid he'd never ask again.

Janine talks of having respect for Gordon and perceiving that he had great potential as a husband. But there was no sense of the love and romance which dominated the music of the day. In the early fifties, the goal of her girlfriends was to receive several proposals of marriage and then rush to be the first at the altar. There was no girlish giddiness or the flashing of an engagement ring for Janine. The wedding was small by prevailing custom, and as some sort of defiant gesture, she bought a wedding gown on sale for forty-two dollars. She remembers she was very analytical about the whole thing.

When they finally made their break to move to British Columbia, Janine received, with mixed feelings, a promise from her father that he would always provide money and tickets back home if she had problems with Gordon. She has thought about the offer since but never accepted it. Possibly the first time was when Gordon lost his first job after six months. A wealthy aunt helped out and Janine went back to university for a teaching degree. She didn't like coming home at the end of the day to hear him on the telephone making job appointments. But she says they were happy. They were far removed from relatives and their advice. They were, as they hoped to be, "anonymous."

But the reality of the situation obviously played havoc with her spirit of rebellion. She is brutally frank in saying that she kept driving Gordon until he was back in engineering. She pushed him into the Rotary Club and the Toastmasters Club, but she could see he was having none of it. Obviously he was not going to stick to any one thing, and it was more complicated than she thought. A fresh start, away from the well-intended interference of their families, had had no effect on Gordon's curious lack of career ambition.

Gordon says: "We have followed this theory of 'you do your thing and I'll do mine.' I would perform admirably at work for about three years and quit. Every job I took was bigger but not more creative. I never felt anything was my own creation." Janine shakes her head and says he quit his jobs without having anything lined up. He actually quit once two weeks before Christmas without even waiting for the bonus. She tried to convince him that he would always find frustrations, but he remained miserable. "Like everything else, I said, 'You'll do what you want to anyway.' He thought he could teach, paint, and do consulting work. I had dreams of him being a struggling artist at home but making enough money so we could have a great life. He's helping me but he's not productive. We haven't had a holiday in three years and it's getting to me. I could never have upgraded myself in my career without him, but now we need more money. He's stuck at home and he's not meeting people."

This is her eternal theme. "What do you mean I don't meet people?" Gordon interjects. "I mean," she says, "that you're quite gregarious in an office." That, Gordon replies, is irrelevant, because he can't play the office game anymore.

Talking to him alone, Gordon settles almost apologetically into a house empty of his children who are at school and his office-going wife. "We always seem to be at a cross-roads," he explains. "I'm convinced I have to be concerned about security. I know you can only play around so long. It's a last-chance type of feeling. I have to admit my painting has become disappointing. There are so many artists and it's tough to make a living. I know it's elitist to pick and choose what you want to do. The problem with being an engineer is that I've never been able to do it the way I want. I won't strive within the system, and when you're older it's demanded of you. I know all my peers are critical of my stance. I think some people feel I'm foolish, that I don't act my age. For some people, if you have a successful business you can measure your life by it. But that's not right for me. My personal philosophy is that life is a search, and you don't find the answers in business."

Gordon elaborates on his search. It has to do with always questioning. At university, he was never encouraged to be critical. He accepted every word because it was written down in a book by someone wiser than he. He came out of this learning environment feeling positive that books had shown him the way. Once he started working, he could see all sorts of mistakes being made, and he realized very few people concern themselves with a continuing quest for knowledge or spirituality. He knows, with this attitude, he will never get his just reward in the marketplace because he has a commodity people won't purchase. The depressing part of daily business, Gordon feels, is having to slap the client on the back and sell him something that isn't up to his own personal standards. Gordon is a poor liar.

Gordon also worries about how selfish he is being. He could climb back to the top again and start providing some material luxury. Was the hope of finding himself through art too much of a personal extravagance? He provides a partial answer to the query: "When we look at the people who have everything, I think of how strong Janine has become because of our situation. She fights everything artificial around her. We have so much else we share. We meet interesting people. I'm friendly with artists and engineers and people from the university."

Work. Money. They seem to make a terrible litany, but Gordon assures me that their marriage is solid. One of the things he likes best about Janine is that she taught him to be communicative and express his feelings. He has been faithful to her and if he had to put a reason to it, it would be this: "If I had an affair it would have to be so meaningful that it would damage the one relationship that means the most to me." And perhaps there is a clue here to this gentle, apologetic man. His art, all aspects of his life, must have meaning.

Shortly after I leave Gordon at their home I meet Janine at a Greek restaurant not far away because she wants to clarify a few things on her own. After another good day at work, she is enthusiastic. She loves encouraging children and bringing out the best in them. She describes herself in this situation as an actress with great sensitivity. That ability, she explains, is why she's good at what she does. She appears quite flamboyant right now. Her mass of curly black-gray hair is being tossed with some vivacity on her part. Her dark eyes are alive. The waiter knows her and flirts a touch; that's life-affirming for Janine. She is, for this moment, an older woman who would be noticed in a roomful of more obviously beautiful women. She struggles—and wins the battle—not to ask me what Gordon said to me in private. I admire this quality of respect.

Well, she announces, her eyes flashing, she is quite disappointed that Gordon doesn't stick with his art. He has so much talent, if only he would use it. If he wrote a book, she says, flinging her hands, she guarantees it would be fabulous. He could do anything if he set his mind to it. "But the truth is," she says with equanimity, "I'll be working until I'm sixty-five years old, no matter what."

Gordon, she continues, is a perfectionist. But if he could ease off a little she could see him as a very successful magazine illustrator. "If I had been his agent instead of his wife, I could have sold him. I don't think he has an answer to the work he wants, and that's a disappointment I'm learning to live with. I keep thinking he will find his perfect situation, and he will be successful and make money, and we'll enjoy ourselves. He's an enigma but he's very interesting. He's such a delightful, wonderful human being. He's a great companion, husband, father, and friend. He just needs somebody to take care of his financial means. He really needs a *patron*."

She has reached a conclusion: The most important thing is for a person to feel successful within himself. This she understands about Gordon. But still, why does it continue to bother her that Gordon is not productive just now? This doesn't mean being rich, she points out. But she would like a weekend at the Bayshore Inn in Vancouver. She is tired of hand-me-down carpets and sick of relatives who buy her things. Dreaming, she would like two weeks in San Francisco, and she would like to go to Europe, the way they did one prosperous year.

Transcendental Meditation has helped her deal with the fact that she's tough and he's not. And the kids fall somewhere in between. TM slows her down when she knows she is being too much of a whirlwind. She demands a great deal of herself, and gets things done even if she has to be blunt and step on a few toes. In contrast, she tells me, what particularly endears her husband to her is that he won't do anything that could possibly cause the slightest hurt to anyone else. He's too *damn* giving. All his friends and acquaintances get his professional advice free. Maybe if he charged for what he counsels over the telephone . . .

Janine cannot see herself married to anyone else. She attributes a great deal of her personal growth to Gordon. She looks at her sister, who married a rich lawyer and has all the possessions, and she says she wouldn't trade places for anything. She's envious, sure, but Gordon gives her the freedom to be herself. That means more. She sometimes has twinges about being aggressive and totally open—too open for some people. But Gordon never accuses her of being a nag. He usually describes her blatant comments as "encouragement."

She tells me something privately that Gordon told me hours earlier. It is one more example of how different they are, and yet attuned. She says both of them now wish they had had sex with each other and other partners before they married. And both of them wish they had traveled and learned more about the world.

Janine thinks she could handle casual affairs but she has never tried, perhaps because of Gordon's loyalty. She has playfully suggested that it might be great if they both have affairs—for the experience and the physical pleasure. He told her that wouldn't work for them, and she has listened even though there are times when an affair seems an acceptable option. They are very loving and take showers together. I tell her that's quite a compliment to her body, if nothing else. "Do you really think so? Isn't this a usual thing for everybody?" Sometimes she reads articles and wonders if she has missed out on a great passion. In the end, she doesn't really think she would be different sexually with another man. "The truth is, I don't really have the capacity to zero in on the sex act." She's usually thinking of a dozen other things. "You know what? I think sex is overrated for very active career people."

The fact that she pushes for more financial security is

really a surface desire. As different as Gordon and Janine are, they are together on the main issue: "Our goals are the very same. We are working toward developing ourselves as good human beings. We are totally honest in all we do. Most people have secrets. We have none."

Janine and Gordon's story has no predictable ending. There was such a mixture of joy and disappointment. But there was in every day a measure of dignity and under-standing. Her turn to have an excellent listener; his turn to have a wonderer. Gordon is totally in the sometimes cruel thrust of the Gauguin Syndrome. But he may very well be-come the artist who lives within. Janine, I'm sure, will always manage, even if she doesn't get her weekend at the Bayshore Inn.

9

Intimate Partners
Working Together

A social worker I know says that couples who work together are a very select group who manage to mesh together completely. Those who don't won't last. He believes one element for their success is the ability to maintain a degree of separateness; in fact, this is as essential for them as being together is for the majority of partners who work apart. "I think these couples are bright, perceptive, and especially creative because they need to be able to tell each other new things. Somehow they've worked out a fifty-fifty balance in sharing the load and it's really noticeable if one breaks the rules."

He says the great advantage is that one partner is not dependent on the other to bring in the outside world, as often happens in relationships where the wives stay at home.

The working couples I talked to are with each other far more hours than most people could stand, but what makes it good for them is their devotion to their individual skills and commonly held goals. They are really working for their mutual benefit. They have picked up certain courtesies; for instance, they know when the other needs to be alone. They also have a high degree of creativity, which allows them to remain excited and stimulated by each other.

The creative insurance that Cindy and Brad, both psychologists at a western Canadian university, took out on their marriage was that they deliberately chose different fields of research, not so estranged that they couldn't understand what the other was trying to achieve but complementary enough that what one was learning sometimes helped the other. They also have different philosophical approaches to their work, and these dissimilarities, combined with a total respect for moments of privacy, seem to nullify the inherent risks that come with working next door to each other, sharing the same colleagues, and going home to the same two small precocious children. When they invited me to share the afternoon and dinner with them, I wasn't sure beforehand whether to classify the interview as one with experts on coupling, or as one with a couple who might give me a glimpse into their study of each other. They functioned in both spheres, beautifully.

As Cindy and I relaxed with wine in their glassed-in sunroom, Brad checked the roast and prepared the vegetables. There were two things that impressed me about their ritual. Unlike some couples who share the duties and pleasures of the household, there was no clear line between his role in the household and hers. There was absolute harmony in the preparation and serving of the meal—no hand signals, no reminders —and best of all, I wasn't left sitting alone for those inevitable last ten minutes when a couple put everything together in the kitchen. Brad and Cindy took turns talking to me while they worked, and when dinner arrived, it seemed to get there without either having done more than the other.

We began talking about the Me Generation, specifically a situation we have all seen around us: couples who have been married twenty years, and are already in their forties, when they suddenly realize they're still young. And that's when they're likely to dwell on what they've missed. It's not as if that particular age group has been hit any harder than any other by the emphasis on personal pleasure and self-knowledge, but their stories do tend to be more urgent and poignant. Cindy says these people irritate her. "How boring to seek yourself and to shut out the rest of life." The essential questions have never varied: Who am I? Why am I here? This is introspection a thinking man can't escape but it has plummeted into narcissism and Brad wonders if we won't end up with a procession of old bitter people living solitary lives.

As psychologists, current social phenomena haven't escaped Brad and Cindy's notice, and we touched on a few of the problems, beginning with the material comfort of the middle class, which has greatly reduced the need for a large and protective family circle. Affluence has also limited the appeal of religions that stress the importance of life after death to compensate for the sufferings on earth. Technology, whether we call it a dishwasher or a laser beam, has made it increasingly possible to enjoy more comfort for less effort. Movies and television allow us to jettison emotions and guilt about wars, pestilence, and childhood horrors because we need only observe and never participate. Popular songs make it unnecessary to explain the facts of life. Rather than making intelligent decisions, one experiences and quickly moves on to sensations for their own sake, and the efficient media quickly spread the word of the new disposable pleasures. Then there is the fact that children well into their twenties are still attending school because there really is no place else for them to go. They learn the pleasures of adult life without having to take on any of the traditional responsibilities. They feel, as many of us do, that there are no great discoveries or adventures left. The individual, compared with the wonders of technology, seems relatively minor in importance. From these broad concerns, we moved into Brad and Cindy's personal sphere.

During their ten years of marriage Brad and Cindy have considered the alternatives—such as open marriage—from both a professional and a personal viewpoint and have dismissed them. They feel their relationship is successful because they got a lot of flings out of the way before they married. Both had serious love affairs in their twenties and they know now that if they had married those people, they would be on their second marriages. By the time they came together, they were mature and had standards they expected of themselves and each other. They had been living together and neither of them was pressing for marriage, but there were two overriding factors: Cindy's mother would never be content until they made it legal and they wanted children. They spent some time studying in England and when they returned to Canada, they decided to give Cindy's mother the ceremony she had set her heart on. Cindy says: "I cared enough to do that for her. I bought the whole bit—the church and the gown and the sycophantic minister. It didn't cost me much in terms of my own values and I'm glad I did it. The only reason I took Brad's name was because my maiden name was very boring."

Even though they were from the same city and won scholarships to the same American university, it was years before they went together. They date the beginning of their romance to a summer they drove back home from university. "We were isolated from the rest of the world and it seemed like a classic novel. We got along so well and we were both interested in everything about psychology. I certainly fancied him but I didn't think he felt the same way."

They clearly enjoy reminiscing about their romance and it is evident they agree on most things and continue to get along well. Brad is very tall, handsome, and bearded and Cindy matches him in attractiveness, intelligence, and gentleness—a dramatic contrast to the flaming temper she displays when the need arises. She has a fighting spirit no one could miss and there is no question she is on equal footing with any man. Brad makes a joke that, aside from the fact she is a psychologist, he likes "her chest." This leads to requisite remarks on women's liberation. Cindy never had the need for a supportive organization. She set her goals early and encountered no real obstacles along the way. Her role model was her father, who, according to her description and Brad's, was the crusading newspaperman who never made it in the big cities but cared for his community. Cindy's mother was a nurse and had to bail out the family during times of financial strain. Cindy was obviously bright and her mother told her in public school that she had to have a career. "She told me, 'You don't have to be stuck.' She pointed out the local belle, who got married and had six kids, a smelly house, and a husband who left her. My mother took pains to explain I had choices open to me." She decided she was going to be a lawyer but she changed her career plans twice for no significant reasons. She went into psychology because a friend told her the professor was fabulous. That was her stumbling entrance into a career that turned out best for her.

Their children, a boy, six, and a girl, four, come in shyly, both of them blond and delicate of feature. Brad is demonstrative with them and shows no impatience when they interrupt the conversation. He kisses Cindy's hand and leaves to make the salad. Cindy is fond but deliberate in her approach to them. She listens to them carefully and encourages them to think of games that each can play if they aren't getting along at the moment. After they leave the room, she says she would rather see them live with someone than marry under the influence of romance. Marriage is serious and for life, and romance is casual. She would discourage anyone under the age of twenty-five from getting married. At a certain age, she says, young people need sex and she would rather see them satisfy that urge than marry the wrong person. Surprisingly, since she grew up in the mid-fifties, when the moral code was strict, she had no soda-fountain-date concept of sex; she wasn't saving *it* for marriage because if and when that came about, she would be older and established in her profession. Her first sexual encounter took place in her teens and she remembers it as being just fine and that the boy had a nice body. She didn't feel guilty about the experience.

When Cindy and Brad married their careers were established and they wanted children. It was difficult finding a suitable housekeeper and, for perhaps the first time, Cindy felt guilty: "We went to work and we left our children with an utterly competent person and yet the guilt of the middle class in this area was overwhelming." She laughs and says that middle-class academics like themselves tend to get silly about their kids.

Brad is quick to dismiss any sign of gratuitous guilt: "Cindy has always been a first-rank academic and I'd no sooner tell her to give up her career than I would my colleague down the street. I don't think it's likely that the children are damaged by this. I know about real damage; about people who have more kids than they can handle; about men who can't stand it and break under the pressure."

Cindy says with the bluntness that one comes to expect from her that fashionable views about raising children are "crap." She says all you have to do is be *reasonable*.

Brad elaborates: "You try to turn the child into a rational creature, a self-evolving entity. You teach him how to avoid failure and how to achieve his own potential. The child is a rational person and his model must be that of a rational adult."

Cindy adds that a child must also see himself as a member of a wider community: his own self-fulfillment can't be paramount.

People are being told the reason they're unhappy is that they don't know who they are. Brad says this is a cruel hoax, because "self-realization is a process that takes a lifetime. You'll know who you are when you're old—and not before. So in the meantime get about the business of life. You'll find freedoms, duties, opportunities, and strengths and talents. And you'll find that the world is infinitely more important than you or I. You can fail from not trying enough or from trying too much without wisdom. You will also find there is absolutely no way you can get through life without making serious mistakes."

Cindy and Brad take marriage *very* seriously and believe that if you are prepared for it, there is every possibility of its being a lifelong commitment. They say it is important to have a sustained relationship before marriage so you know you are compatible partners and not just starry-eyed lovers. They say women, in particular, can survive without a husband until they learn how the world works.

Brad says there is no scientific evidence of any essential differences in the functioning of male and female brains, and career opportunities must be equal. Equal rights is a movement that won't be stopped, but both are aware that one of the bad side effects of women's liberation is that some women feel guilty because they enjoy being housewives.

Although Brad and Cindy work together every day, they have different areas of interest. Brad's is the theory of knowledge and Cindy is concerned with the philosophy of language. What they have in common, Brad says, is "how the machinery between your ears works. We complement each other in a deliberate way and we have a research program that will take us the rest of our lives to pursue. Our common concern is how the brain's understanding of the universe grows and improves at the individual and cultural level. We keep up with each other's work and we constantly teach each other. We're very fortunate. I am successful in ways I couldn't be without her." Cindy, looking pleased, says Brad's thoughts are always fresh and imaginative.

They have been lucky in their lives and in their choice of each other. There has been no crisis—no financial hardship, no death or serious illness or a relative coming to live with them. There has also been no infidelity. Brad attempts to make light of the possibility of Cindy having an affair by saying he watches Cindy "like a hawk." He knows that she is attractive, intellectually and physically, and she has opportunities to meet other men. "I would be caught completely off guard because her office *is* next door to mine. The time we don't spend together is very small. I just wouldn't believe it for a moment. I guess I could live with something like that; it's not the grounds for ending the whole thing. I believe in monogamy and I personally don't have any difficulty with it. How easy it is for a

man to be unfaithful will depend on how big a hold his fantasies have on him and how much he got out of his system before marriage. No mystery beckons me because I've had romance. Our first spring together was delightfully romantic and
indulgent. It was like a brief froth and then the marriage
evolved. It will be different five or ten years from now because
we are evolving together." He turns to Cindy and tells her she
is not the same anymore but that he feels they are closer than
they could have ever foreseen. They go to conferences by
themselves—a possible occasion for an affair—but he doesn't
think either of them worries about it. Cindy also has close platonic relationships with some men and Brad says it would take
a lot to make him jealous at this stage. He likes her choice of
friends and congratulates her for not bringing home "bone-
heads or dogs."

Cindy, however, *does* think about Brad having an affair;
it's not something that automatically slips from your mind just
because it hasn't happened so far. She imagines that she could
deal with it, but not, she says vehemently, if it were one of his
freshman students. "A one-night stand is kinder," she says,
"but I still wouldn't like it."

Brad assures her with amusement: "That's sweet of you.
My love for you has the nature of shoe leather. It can stand a
few kicks." Some people have frankly wondered how their
marriage stays so vital when they are private to begin with and
also have interwoven careers. "Well," Brad answers, "you
don't ever push and you always knock before you ever open
the other's door." They are also perfectly matched in the pleasures they take in their free time. They love books, constant
learning, and stimulating dinner parties at home, and—of
prime importance to them—they truly enjoy making every moment count with their children. Brad expressed best how they
both live. He said: "We really look forward to every day of
our lives together."

*   *   *

   This same outlook toward careers and marriage is shared
by Don and Joanne, who spend almost every hour of every
day with each other. They are members of an orchestra in a
Canadian prairie province and the parents of three young children. They lead an extremely busy life. When they're not playing with the orchestra or on tour, they do guest work with
other groups. But they manage to have time for their children
and for pleasure even though it would seem to be achieved at
times by rigid scheduling. On the surface it is easy to see what
has made it work for them. They are equally respected as
musicians and they are so self-sufficient that they would not
collapse if they were on their own. There is consideration but
no subservient roles in this comfortable household. The first
time I telephoned Don said they had been out late the night
before but he had been up early with the children so Joanne
could sleep until noon.

   We sat in the back yard of their suburban home drinking
beer in the sunshine while the children played about us. Both
Don and Joanne are thirty-five and have been married eleven
years. Don's boyish good looks are curiously accentuated by
a brush cut, which is a rare thing these days and is perhaps a
statement about himself. He is without guile and unconcerned
with any current fashion. He speaks directly, without pause to
consider the effect of his words. The impression is that there is
nothing to hide. A friend had told me that the women in the
orchestra consider him to be "superstraight."

   Joanne's hair is precisely coiffed and sprayed, again not
done in the current vogue. She is easy to talk to but there is the
suggestion that she is very aware of the impressions she is
making. They have created a solid and correct life-style and
they are both proud of the fact that they have done so, since
their backgrounds couldn't be more opposite. This subject
comes up almost immediately when I comment on how polite
their children are and Don says adamantly that he does not believe in spanking. He believes talking and persuasion are bet-

ter. It's not hard to understand why when he adds that his father always hit him with a belt and asked questions later.

From this he skips immediately to the fact that he would not come home to "a dumb wife who does nothing all day." Don knows these attitudes are the legacy of a bleak lower-class childhood in England. His father demanded that he be a carpenter like himself, but Don joined the Air Force instead. Disappointment still festers in the family. His parents have never been in the audience when he has played in an orchestra and he says with undisguised bitterness: "Even if my son is a garbage man, I'll give him the best education for that job and I'll go out and watch him at work. I'll be proud of him." Although his parents have been married for forty years, he says they merely exist together. His mother is stout and constantly eats sweets and, as a result, Don won't touch a dessert. Don is elitist and he knows it when he says he can't help compare his parents, whom he describes as Victorian and poorly educated, with his in-laws, who are university-educated and aware of what is happening in the world. When his parents visit them from England, he says he has to "chaperone" them and the resentment shows through clearly. This successful musician, who restores old violins, lets it drop that he never touched a musical instrument until he was eighteen years old and is almost entirely self-taught.

Joanne had all the advantages. She is a third-generation musician and she knew from the age of ten what she was going to do with the rest of her life. She had a very comfortable and happy childhood and she never had any desire to rebel. "I was a good girl and there was never a question of disobedience." She knew her parents would send her to college and she was encouraged every step of the way to take advantage of her talents. Heeding their advice paid off. She thinks back to university, when most of the girls in her dormitory spent all day Saturday getting ready for their dates. Their thoughts were all on getting married and they didn't even know whom they were marrying. Joanne thinks it's best when people get married later because women, in particular, have a far better chance to establish their goals. She says she and Don are living exactly like her parents. "My mother," she explains, "is very determined and my father is very diplomatic. She seems stronger but he's the final authority. I had the example of a strong family relationship. They always agreed. It was a partnership between the two of them. I honestly never saw a fight between my parents. They have a very traditional marriage and present a united front."

They talk of the breakup of some of their colleagues' marriages and think that a fundamental problem is that one partner tries to make the other fit into a pattern. When people merely live together, the tendency is for them to try to please one another, but once they are married, the fifty-fifty sharing rapidly becomes forty-sixty or less. But Don and Joanne believe compromise has to be accepted graciously. In one given situation, one partner is going to take and the other is going to receive; in another, the reverse is true. The trouble begins when the taking becomes one-sided and one person is always demanding more. Joanne says Don accepts the maxim that you have to work hard at marriage, but she doesn't. She is not aware that her parents, who are still happily married, consciously worked at it. Still, she has seen people who don't try anymore and she feels sorry for them. Possibly because she is talented and self-assured, she regards them with a clinician's dispassionate reserve. She talks about an acquaintance whose husband still looks the same as he did when they married, but she weighs two hundred pounds and talks about nothing but doing the family laundry and television soap operas. If she wants to stay home that's fine, Joanne says, but she has let herself down by not keeping herself in shape, by not being interested in her husband's career, and by regressing to the point where she can't discuss anything outside her own four walls. "Working women have to get dressed up and be decent and pleasant," she says. "Men have always had to toe the line. They've had to be alert and ready for work."

Don suggests it would be better if more women knew what they wanted to do before they got married; too many of them fall into careers or jobs that they may not like or be suited for. Joanne counters that some men thwart their wives every way they can. They want them to stay at home and are threatened by their independence. Women who are in marriages that make it impossible for them to establish and maintain healthy self-images should leave without any guilt, she says.

Sexual fidelity is a resolved issue with them. Joanne says, practically, that it would be next to impossible for Don to stray since they're together all the time. Don is a little lighter in tone when he says, "I can't get away with a damn thing." Joanne tends to notice the affairs that rip apart other marriages. Don recognizes infidelity as a possibility if couples don't keep the sexual spark alive. If you don't get what you want at home, he says, you look elsewhere because you have only one life to live. "I have a wife and I'm relatively happy but there's always a danger. I watch my colleagues who seem happily married for ten years or more and then they're fooling around and looking for something better. The other woman might do something better than your wife—and then what do you do?"

Joanne informs him that even if someone else is very attractive, the commitment is to the marriage vow. Plain and simple. Although she meets more men than many other women do she makes it clear that she is neither single nor available. The men she knows are instantly put into the category of friend and there's nothing at all difficult about doing this. It's very admirable to be so tidy about your emotions, Don says, but he wonders how many men are as capable and strong as she seems to be. In the end, their perception is that sexual experimentation usually ends in chaos. This is what happened to a couple they know who married after living together compatibly for six years. They had discussed a sexually open marriage and although she was reluctant, the husband assumed he had her approval. She walked out for good the day he asked her to leave her own house so he could have intercourse with an old friend. "If you live together that long, you'd think they would know what the reaction would be to such an agreement," Don says. "But it's always the male ego. A man is afraid of losing his virility. It's almost inevitable for men to want to try other women at a certain age. I haven't had that crisis but I know a lot of people who have. I wonder how they can go back to their wives afterwards. I'd have guilt written all over my face. I don't know how you could ever say to your wife again, 'Darling, I love you.'"

Traditional roles in marriage have changed, particularly for career couples, and they support the idea that a husband can no longer assume that he dictates where the family will live. They have been lucky to be accepted together in the same orchestras but they can't expect this to continue forever. There is always the specter of only one of them being offered an excellent musical position in a different city. In such a situation, a tremendous sacrifice would be required and I suspect from the way they speak about their careers that it would be harder for Joanne to accept a move someplace else because of an offer Don had.

They described how they apportion their time, the hours that go into practice, tours, guest appearances, the children, the essential private time when Joanne sews and Don makes furniture. Joanne does the housework once a week and Don handles the outside chores. If things pile up, they work together to rush through the work. They usually work at night, so the children have dinner with them and they can enjoy being a family and sharing the things that matter to them.

But when it comes to their feelings about their careers as members of the orchestra, I think I am correct in suspecting there is an absolute limit to Joanne's willingness to compromise. "I have to be very careful how I say this. I can keep up with all my career obligations and feel that I am not sacrificing someone else's well-being. I teach students and I could have more of them but I don't. I can cut down on that—but *nothing else!*"

Don, describing the same artistic happiness, also says that being tied down by a mortgage and marriage and kids is a "privileged responsibility. You have to decide what is important, the job you do or the life you live. I love my work but it's a means to an end—the support of my family." He never forgets that he earns money doing what pleases him the most, just as he never forgets an old tradesman who told him he had held his job for thirty-five years and hated every minute of it. The problem, as Don sees it, is that too many people don't choose the right thing to do with their lives. Then they feel they don't have enough in life, and part of the blame can be placed on the media for propagating the ridiculous notion of limitless well-being. "There's so much selfishness today," he says. "Success used to mean you worked and built together. I hope this idea comes back."

Don and Joanne have not looked beyond their own talents and hard work for the success or comfort they have achieved. Joanne is professional, she's competitive, and she has never felt any discrimination being a female member of an orchestra. However, there are a few women musicians who Don says give women's liberation a bad name. "They can be a pain in the neck on tour because they seem to think they have to prove themselves by going to bed with the players." He has empathy for homosexual rights. "I have worked with famous homosexuals and they're always getting creamed by people like Anita Bryant. Do we junk genius because of different sexual feelings? I say live and let live."

Very early in our conversation, Joanne had expressed a fear that some men undergo sudden and drastic changes in the midpoint of their lives. This worries her because she and Don want things to stay the way they are. They've had their gypsy years of traveling and establishing themselves and they have had to forge their particular means of dealing with the risks of working and competing and loving all at the same time. For some couples, this would be disastrous. For them it has been a matter of rather fine orchestration.

It seems that the telephone always rings at night just when Tina and Victor are sitting with their feet up, unwinding from another day. But such interruptions come with the territory. They are both lawyers and married to each other.

For most of their eleven married years, Tina and Victor worked together in the same legal offices, and in 1971, they opened their own firm in Toronto and became equal partners. But equality can backfire. There was Tina one weekend, with a six-week-old child, handling an injunction against a large union, and in walked the big union boys, straight into her kitchen. There she was holding a baby under her arm and walking up and down, asking questions and reading the law to them. "Afterwards," Tina says, "Victor and I sat down on the front steps and asked each other if we really wanted to live this way." They decided right then that what mattered most was each other, their children, and their home, and that they would try to practice good law second. Tina made another rule: No legal discussions after 10 P.M. They have kept all of these resolves save one: Victor still talks about his cases in bed.

They met at law school and married after Tina's graduation. When Victor graduated a year later he had many offers but decided to join the firm where she was working. This would cause many people to think twice, but not Tina. She believes that a man or a woman must be very lonely if a spouse doesn't comprehend what he or she is doing. This meshes nicely with Victor's point of view: "Litigation is demanding and there is an emotional price. It's nice to be married to someone who understands. It's mostly hard slugging but sometimes there is some glamor. If things have gone well in court and Tina comes home feeling very up, I know her feeling exactly. I can also sympathize when she comes home with her tail behind her."

The fact that Victor's name is listed before Tina's on their legal firm has nothing to do with male chauvinism. They both agree that it just sounded better. And there is no particular reason why Tina has never used her married name. It was never an issue, but now that she is professionally recognized, she wouldn't change it. They didn't establish the firm to be together but rather as a chance for them to advance equally. They specialize in independent cases of child representation and child abuse, and they had a head start in a burgeoning field. They're known around the courts as "Mr. and Mrs. Child Rep."

The reason Tina, who is thirty-seven and two years younger than Victor, imposed the nightly curfew on legal discussions is that they always seem to be talking about the law. For them it's a whole philosophical area and every case is different. Often one is dealing with a point of law or a set of circumstances that can inform and help the other. A distinct advantage is that they can take each other's cases if one of them can't be in court at a certain time. Victor says they make a point of telling clients that not only are they partners but they're married, and if one is going to substitute for the other they're both filled in on the details.

Tina says they complement each other and she has little tolerance for the notion that she and Victor compete. "If you're working toward a common goal, I don't think there has to be competition between partners. Victor also dismisses any idea of competitiveness. "I'm a good lawyer. She's a good lawyer. Tina doesn't lose many cases and if it does happen, I have never said: 'Gee, if she had done this or that it would have worked out better.'" Although they share the same office space, they have their separate clients and while they may literally bump into each other in the same courthouse, they never appear in the same courtroom. In fact, they have never even seen each other in action. It smacks of checking up, and the idea is abhorrent to them.

Their days take considerable planning, particularly because of their daughters, who are four, seven, and eight years of age. Both partners are in court almost every day, and while their office hours end at five-thirty, someone has to be home by five to take over from the babysitter and see that the children get to their swimming, ballet, and music lessons. Inevitably, Tina and Victor spend at least an hour after the family's dinner reviewing the next day's cases, and they're rarely in bed before midnight. In order to give more time to their children, they have stopped seeing clients on weekends, and the past few summers they have closed the firm for five weeks and rented a cottage where they couldn't be reached by telephone. It's all a matter of priorities, because the clients will eat up all their time if they let them. "It's not a case of saying I wish I were the greatest lawyer in Canada," Victor explains. "We're good at what we do but our family means more to us than the practice of a business." Because they handle children's cases, they believe they have a deeper appreciation and understanding of their own children. "You really wonder how a kid who is abused and deprived holds together so well," Tina says. "I have seen some real survivors. We talk a lot to psychologists and psychiatrists and it helps in our personal life to have information on the family and the tensions that can be created."

As far as they are concerned, working together is a personal and professional bonus, but they can imagine the day when one or both want to try something new. In the meantime, Tina says: "We have had to recognize that each of us must put in a fifty-fifty effort at work and at home and that's difficult to achieve. When a woman stays at home she is putting in a twenty-four-hour day while her husband is putting in eight hours. There's an inequality here and I think this takes a lot of sorting out in every marriage. It's essential that you both develop the right attitude. For us everything seems to work out without any great discussion." They draw equal salaries from the firm, keep separate bank accounts, and make purchases by mutual agreement. They're willing to trade time for the money they could be making so they can take the children on frequent trips. They've considered a vacation for just the two of them but they've never done this because Tina says it's exciting to see things through the eyes of children.

Victor says that people are always telling him that they'll become overexposed to each other and bored. But the reality is this: "I saw Tina walk out the door this morning and I didn't see her again until five o'clock tonight. Sometimes we barely cross each other's paths." They feel it's too easy to get trapped into an isolated circle that involves only home and work and so they also have separate, outside activities; to name only two, he's with a ratepayers' association and she's on the Canadian Opera Company's women's committee. There is a constant flow of new people and new ideas. Because of her profession, Tina points out that she spends a great deal of time with other men and Victor merely laughs at this: "If you can squeeze in an affair, good luck to you." The fact is that they were mature and established when they married and their sexual flings were in the past. They are, very naturally, monogamous and their trust in each other is implicit. They can't conceive of losing so much affection for each other that an affair would be possible.

Tina thinks about her life with Victor and says: "We are quite different people but we share a common attitude toward life. If this attitude exists in a marriage, I don't see that working at the same kind of career would ever cause problems."

10

And God Makes Three
Religion in Marriage

This chapter deals with the role that God, or spirituality, can
play in the lives of couples who stay together. In today's
world, they often feel like outsiders, somewhat strange or
prissy. It may be *au courant* to mention in passing that your
adolescent daughter is on the Pill—and what can you do about
it? But it can be disturbing to the social ambience to suggest
that you believe in God or go to church. One may be titillated
by the former; one is more likely to be embarrassed by the
latter.

Nevertheless, there is the gentle reality, which seems to
occupy small space in the social rooms of our lives, that more
people than we realize are held together by a belief in the existence of something grander than themselves. A strong belief
in God does not necessarily keep them in harmony but many
couples who have it say it adds a dimension to their togeth-
erness.

There are periodic surveys showing that a majority of
people profess religious beliefs and that God is not necessarily
a Sunday kind of love. A 1980 *Ladies' Home Journal* poll of
thirty thousand women reported that 47.7 per cent were moderately religious and 16.5 per cent were very religious. Many
of the people I interviewed expressed a belief in God and the
importance of raising children with moral and social values,
but often this was mentioned only for a few minutes. But

whatever their feelings about organized religion or the gods of the East or West, they wanted their children to *believe*. Believe in what? Decency, for sure. Some will pass on strict religious values and rituals and risk rejection by their children in a modern world; others hope their children will perceive their parents as *good* people and follow suit. No survey has established which group will be more successful.

In this chapter we are dealing with people's lives which are totally governed by God. They are proud to stand out from the crowd. They are not "religious fanatics" but normal, quiet people trying to abide in a spiritual way in a world that seems more than slightly askew.

Marvin and Emma have been married thirty-seven years and have raised six children in a staunchly Roman Catholic household, even though Emma isn't herself a devout Catholic. She has worked equally with her husband in instilling religious devotion, sending the children off to mass and separate schools, and listening to their catechism lessons. Along with Marvin, she was one of the original organizers of the Marriage Encounter Movement in Canada.

For years they and various nuns and priests have led weekend encounters for couples who want to improve their marriages. Five of their six children have remained strong in the Catholic faith—all of which is a rather unusual report from a United Church woman who has never felt any compelling reason to exchange her peaceful pew in her church for one in the church of her husband and children.

It is Emma's belief in God that motivates her, not the dictates of any religious denomination. There have been some insulting moments when she felt like an outsider but she and her husband have evolved a truly ecumenical life-style, and strong friendships with both Catholic and Protestant clergy.

A high point in both their faith and their marriage came eleven years ago when they attended an organized marriage encounter weekend as a favor to a friend who was leading the group. They felt so revitalized in their own relationship that they readily agreed to join the organization together. They started the first branch of this kind in their home city of Montreal, and over the years led thirty encounter weekends, spreading the word about old and good marriages. Their emphasis is on enhancing communication. One of the methods they use during a weekend is to ask couples to write letters to each other about what they feel is good and bad in their relationship. They work mainly with people who want to stay together but who feel there is something more they can add to their marriages. The couples and the priests who conduct the weekends don't consider themselves as experts, but rather as "enablers."

One of the problems today, Emma feels, is that there is too much emphasis on professional counseling. Couples are made to feel they are incapable of working things out for themselves. Marvin says some couples can only recognize problems and have decided that marriage is a problem in itself. Basically, they still have a foundation to build on but they need a new outlook. They fall into habits that eventually they consider to be a right, even if it makes someone else uncomfortable. Perhaps one partner begins every serious conversation by dictating how things are going to be from now on. This can be erosion of a deadly kind. Emma and Marvin want couples to realize this, but their encounters are the nonabrasive kind. No primal screaming or hurled accusations, but the dawning of an essential perception: perhaps your way isn't always the only answer, perhaps a discussion of the options and compromise isn't anathema to love. It is rewarding work for Emma and Marvin. They speak of the times people have told them they didn't realize their spouses still loved them—after all these years. Emma knows the feeling. She remembers her marriage encounter so many years ago: "We didn't understand that we had any problems with communication, that we could sharpen our responses. It was so rewarding for me as a middle-aged woman—and all that entails—to realize that things could be as good as ever."

Now in their sixties, they live in a big comfortable home with a daughter who is engaged to be married. All their children have stayed home until they married. This is proof for them of their belief that as long as things go right with a couple, so goes the family. When they met, Emma only went to Christmas services at the United Church. Marvin's intense Catholicism was such an integral part of his personality that she saw it as both a strength and a potential source of conflict. "Religion," she says, "seemed to mean more to him and not so much to me, and so it wasn't hard to make the promise to raise our future children in his faith. After our first child was born, Marvin said he thought I should go back to my own church for six weeks and I did. It didn't do anything for me. Maybe we were both concerned because I had an emergency cesarean section and our baby was very sick. When our second child came along, things were fine. Gradually I started to go back to the United Church. Over the years, I received a lot of strength and comfort. I hoped I wouldn't be bitter or resentful of Roman Catholics because the church was very condescending to me in those days because of our mixed marriage. You can imagine how I felt when my children came home and said they were praying for my conversion at school. There always seemed to be a priest saying he hoped I would get the faith. But that was a long time ago. I took instructions to understand the Catholic Church and I have become a sort of authority. I feel the Lord will call me if he wants. In the meantime I'm comfortable in my own church."

Marvin has never felt he wanted to convert Emma. He says, unequivocally, that he is a better Catholic because of her. This, he feels, has come from having to think out their positions more than if they belonged to the same faith. He says his children are better off for being aware of two points of view. As an example, he says one of their rituals was to have leisurely Sunday lunches when they compared their experiences after attending different church services. An inevitable topic of conversation, as their children reached adolescence, was birth control. Emma laughs about this. The Catholic-approved rhythm method worked just fine for her: she wanted a large family anyway.

Things are different now, Marvin points out. From an absolute and inflexible stand that sex and procreation are inseparable, the church has moved toward accepting the planning of children as a matter of conscience for individual couples. As he sees it, you can live without much money but you must be able to love the children you bring into the world. He recognizes that some people's love stretches only so far. Emma notes a stingy attitude among some couples who have decided not to have children, or who look aghast at people who give birth to more than the requisite girl for Daddy and boy for Mommy. She says they are denying themselves "God's greatest gift"—a joyful family.

Emma and Marvin are articulate and unembarrassed talking about their dependence on God and faith in a cultural atmosphere that appears, on the surface, to be almost horrifyingly secular and self-serving. Marvin is far more biblical, quoting scripture and sounding prophet-full of patience for a wayward world. Emma tends to search out the "joyful" experiences of life. But she is earthbound enough to speak against the potential injustices of religious rigidity, and some of her own hurts. She's willing to talk about feeling excluded because she's not the same faith, even though she has worked more for the Catholic Church than the average member in good standing. She's willing to face the appalled expressions on the faces of "liberated" women when she tells them she had all six children by cesarean birth, and used the rhythm method when she's not even a Catholic. She also believes that divorce is essential. Essential because of brutalities, fatefully wrong or youthfully misguided choices, and, occasionally, for the sake of sanity when nothing has worked, when you find yourself disappearing beyond the grasp of life with a partner for whom you have been dead for years.

Forgiveness is at the root of all religious beliefs and Marvin accepts that a person must try to forgive and forget all hurts, even up to marital infidelity. If couples can work this through, he believes they have a chance of getting back together on a stronger and higher level. But if they stay together and one wants to make the other pay, it is, as Emma points out, "hell for two." People have often told Marvin that they can forgive but they can never forget. He tells them: "The basis of a good marriage is love and it is selfless. If you feel all the time that you have been wronged, then you are denying any love that was ever there." Emma would like to see it become harder to get married and easier to divorce. So many people have no idea what they are getting into. But if they make a mistake, they should be able to divorce without recrimination from church or society. Emma says: "I don't think the Lord expects you to pay for a mistake forever."

Marvin remembers when one of their daughters was engaged and both he and Emma were convinced she had made the wrong choice. While many parents tend to stay out of their grown children's lives—if only because they were told years ago to mind their own business because they couldn't possibly understand—Marvin stated his misgivings and asked her to wait for one year. At the end of that time, she broke off the relationship and, Marvin says, in the light of what kind of husband the man turned out to be to another woman, his daughter is glad she did.

All through their growing years, they taught their children that marriage was not to be entered into lightly, and that sex shouldn't be casual and isolated from committed love. Emma offers herself as an example: "I had my children over a twelve-year period and the older ones knew me when I was pregnant. They saw it as a part of life when otherwise they may have developed the idea that sex can be separate from a family life."

While some other couples worry about the quality and frequency of their orgasms and whether or not they're compromising too much of themselves in a relationship, Marvin and Emma have moved quietly along, recognizing that spirituality is at the core of their love. They say any experience of love has to be an experience of God. Spirituality gives that added dimension to life and Emma wishes her eighty-five-year-old mother were more familiar with it. Her mother has gone to church all her life but she does not have a deep understanding of God and, according to Emma, nothing extra to sustain her in the final years of life. Their unshakable values have been passed on to their children, although they accept that there is little they can do about outside influences. They just hope that their children have been made strong by their faith. They have never watered down their version of the truth to suit the changing times. They have never held with allowing a child to make up his mind about religion when he's older—any more than they would allow a child to decide when he needs to see a doctor or a dentist.

They have controlled what happens within their own house and who is allowed to be part of it. There were times when they had to explain to their children that their friends had ideas they didn't approve of. But they never ordered them not to see them again. Marvin and Emma have never been afraid of being labeled judgmental and their children's friends had to accept that theirs was a *religious* home. "Our children are entitled to a clear statement of what we believe and expect from them," Marvin says. "Later on they can reject it if they want. All parents can do is pass on what they have and pray it's useful in the development of the child. If you give them the impression you're wishy washy, you deprive them. If they don't see you for or against an issue, they feel no need to take a stand either."

The accumulation of money has never been a part of their lives, and this sets them apart from much of the neighborhood. When their friends were taking summer jobs to buy bicycles and records, Marvin and Emma encouraged their children to do volunteer work, especially at camps for the retarded. This shunning of luxuries went so far that Emma, with all the dirty dishes left by six kids, never accepted her husband's offer of a dishwasher. She told him more good was accomplished by sharing household tasks.

Emma started out her marriage by thinking she wanted four children. When she had four, she says, it didn't seem like very many. She had her last two children when she was close to forty years old and all her friends kept saying "Poor you," but she didn't agree. She does not understand her women friends who tell her they're too old to have children when they're not much beyond the age of thirty. She says having children up to age forty is fine, and she doesn't believe that the risks of defective children are so high that she shouldn't gamble for the joy.

Certainly the children have kept her tied down and she's aware that she must seem very traditional and unliberated to others. But being at home most of the time didn't mean she lacked growth, like some flower deprived of sunshine. She knows some women need their self-esteem raised by having careers but this wasn't true for her. Her husband says all people have roles to play and he has never felt superior to any woman. From the early days of their marriage, Marvin shared the cooking and cleaning. For a time when Emma worked in a factory during the war, she earned more money than he did. He describes this period as "my training in humility." Emma says her role as a neighborhood mother and a volunteer was more valuable than any of the paychecks she once earned. People have questioned her about not exploiting her potential talent in the marketplace but she feels she has put it into better service. There were so many times she was glad to be home. She mentions how one of her sons told her he didn't think abortion was such a big issue. "I told him I went to bed for nine weeks to preserve him when I was pregnant and started to bleed. I told him I didn't regard him as a nonissue. This forced him to consider what he was saying."

Emma and Marvin are convinced that many marriages are better than most people think. Sometimes we all wish things were different and it's difficult, as Emma says, to realize in mundane circumstances how lucky we are. Emma can remember how her mother complained for years about her father's lack of sociability, saying she wished he would go willingly to her functions. Emma finally told her to be grateful that he went anywhere with her at all. For Emma and Marvin, everything must be kept in perspective. This isn't easy to achieve. Just because they have an abiding faith doesn't mean their lives are without tension, sorrow, disappointment, and compromises they have not enjoyed making. But the belief that there is more to life than personal esteem and accomplishments on earth has brought them to a set of rules that work for them. Their children have not been rushed past them or wished away to a certain age when they presumably would be more manageable; they have accepted the turmoil and consider their children, in the end, to be independent and praiseworthy. Marital fidelity, which is on everyone's mind, is a reality and an ideal they hold out as totally possible. They believe sexual infidelity comes about when people cease to work at love. We all change and develop and so should love. People who don't move past the emotional state of romance don't understand that love is a process, not a static condition, and that a rightly placed smile is often worth more than his tongue in your cheek. Emma says: "All the people who are into sensitivity training are looking for a perpetual high that doesn't exist. Certainly we all have high periods but the calm, peaceful life is preferred."

Emma says there is a lot of misunderstanding about the role of sex in marriage. It's a part of the total relationship, but if sex plays an inflated role, you're bound to look elsewhere. She adds that when people reconcile after infidelity, it has usually been the faith and capacity for forgiveness of one partner.

"If you can forgive you can work it out. If it has been a long marriage, there are more things to bind you together." "Bind" is also a four-letter word and more people are rebelling against the idea of staying together for the sake of appearances, or because of moral or legal sanctions. Emma says people who stay together are bound by intangibles which can't be described and "can't be put in a paper bag and weighed."

Marvin believes that if one partner is unfaithful, it doesn't release the other from the vow made at marriage. For him, a worse infidelity is the failure to love, cherish, and care for the other person. "It's natural to have rough periods but the solution is not radical surgery. Divorce as a solution seems contagious. Some people just don't want to endure. They have the habit of settling back and waiting to reap the benefits of the wonderful state of marriage they've been told about. But it's a shock when a man and woman get married. There are adjustments to make every day. Emma and I don't love each other because we made a commitment. I'm free to love her or not. The freer each one of us is the better we can love each other. All I know is that when I found out that I was loved, then I was free."

Nick's wife didn't know he was there, kneeling beside her bed, when she slipped into a coma. She didn't see him raise his fist in the air daring God to prove his existence, and to give some explanation why a beautiful woman in her twenties would be dying of cancer. "I said, 'God, if you're there, help us.' Within moments, inside my head, a voice said, 'Consider the lilies of the field.' I had no Bible learning and it didn't mean anything to me. I asked a neighbor to come and sit with me. She was a woman of tranquillity and she had helped my wife before. I asked where those words came from. She talked to me about the anxieties of life and how God looks after everything. That went to my heart. There was a realization that God knew my innermost thoughts and it broke me. But I was also thinking, 'Not only is my wife dying but what happens to *me?*"

This happened six years ago and it was the beginning of the path to becoming a born-again Christian. But it was hardly Paul's instant conversion on the road to Damascus. Nick lived with a woman several months after his wife's death and, in the beginning, he says it was for the sake of his motherless son and her fatherless daughter. But all the while his conscience and his intellect gave him a bad time. He had always been vehemently against the concept of a God; religions were crutches for people who couldn't stand up for themselves. But no matter how much he railed, he found enormous comfort in the Bible passage about the lilies of the field, how you didn't have to toil because God looks after you. The story of Nick and Marsha, the woman he lived with and eventually married, is complicated and possibly naïve for the sophisticated palate. It involves a return to innocence many of us don't believe in. God, we are told, is an option.

Nick is a television director in Toronto and he was once a thoroughly contemporary man with more options than most. He is hesitant to put it in words, but he was confronted with television groupies who Nick described as "little girls who are very dangerous—as dangerous as you allow them to be." It wasn't that difficult to resist temptation because he had his first wife, a lovely house, a good job, a baby son, and everything going for him until the cancer hit. It took an awful lot of nonsense out of their lives. They had been married for three years and were happy with each other. They had no fantasies about playing around or ending the marriage. In retrospect, it also seems to Nick that they were very materialistic. But once cancer struck nothing else seemed to matter. They had never confronted death and suddenly they were in this strange situation of reaching out to anybody for answers. The doctors, for all their cleverness, could do nothing. They saw no purpose to their lives or the lives of people around them.

The one exception was their neighbor, a woman who had

recently accepted Jesus Christ. She seemed to bring a power and a peace into their house, and she also brought her Bible. "I came home one night," Nick recalls, "and my wife was propped up in bed. She said to me, 'Everything is here,' pointing to the Bible. She came to the Lord the day before she died." In his loneliness and grief, he started to read this book his wife set so much store by.

He remembers the first thing he prayed for was a suitable housekeeper for his young son, and he found one almost immediately. When his hurt lessened, he prayed for someone to love him and his boy. That's when he developed a friendship with Marsha, who was working at the television station. He considered her "a gift from God" and lived with her in his house for three years; her divorce was complicated and hadn't come through yet. Although she was a good mother to her own daughter and his son and he considered her his wife, he thought sometimes they were doing wrong. The fact that they were living common-law preyed on his mind although no one was censuring them, just this inner voice of his. It was so powerful that for the last six months of their relationship, they abstained from sex. Then Nick moved to his parents' house and waited four months until they could be married in a church.

Marsha, who is small, feminine, and very beautiful at the age of thirty-two, had two marriages behind her when she began seeing Nick. She never felt bitter about men even though the only positive thing she can say about her first two husbands was that the first one gave her her daughter, who is now thirteen, and her second husband was at least a decent father to her. What initially drew her to Nick was sympathy about his wife's death and the fact that he too was trying to raise a child alone. What annoyed her about him was his frequent talks about God. Her parents were moral people, but God had nothing to do with her life. In fact, as far as moral values were concerned, they had distinct disadvantages for her; her father drummed it into her that if she had sexual relations with a boy, she was obliged to marry him. So at age sev-

enteen she was forced to marry though she knew it would
never work. That sort of moral interpretation didn't exactly
make her enamored of God.

Marsha can remember times when she demanded of
Nick: "If God is so good, why is your wife dead?" But because
of the strength of Nick's faith and his goodness, she searched
her own heart and read the scriptures to find out what had
such a hold on him. The turning point came when Nick's aunt
was visiting and she belittled religious beliefs. Marsha became
angry and blurted out: "Jesus shed his blood for us." It was, in
effect, her first public acceptance and she still doesn't understand what prompted it. Then a few days later she learned that
her father, an alcoholic with a twenty-five-year marriage in
ruins, had accepted Jesus Christ and returned home to his
wife. "I realized," Marsha says, "that because I spoke up for
Jesus he had blessed my dad. Then I started to think about
Nick and I living together. We talked it over and decided
through prayer that we had to show our obedience to God. It
was the most thrilling moment of our lives. We had to avoid
the appearance of evil and we had to accept the fact that our
family would have to be separated for a while. The Lord
showed me that as a divorced woman I could marry again. He
gave me the scripture where King David committed adultery
and was forgiven. What I had done was in the past and it was
all forgiven. I was like a new creature."

Christian fervor notwithstanding, it was hard for both of
them when Nick walked out the door of their century-old
house with his vegetable garden and the barn for the horse and
pony he had given Marsha's daughter. They spent a last weekend together praying and fasting, and then Marsha told him to
go. The children were laughing and crying but they were being
raised as Christians, and it had been explained to them that
their parents should not have lived together in the first place.
Nick would be back to visit until it was right for them to be together again.

They have been married four years now and there is

enormous love and unity. But their belief in self-denial and obedience has intensified the usual compromises of marriage. Nick explains. "One day we had a real row. We've had several because we're not angels and we still have a lot of selfishness. But I knew I was right in this situation. I was driving to work with my guts in a knot and I felt bitter about Marsha. Then I remembered that God says I am to love my wife and I felt a great peace. Accepting Jesus Christ is life-changing. It comes from the heart, not the head."

And the life-changing isn't without its penalties. They have lost previously close friends because they are so preoccupied with spiritual matters. They are outgoing and like to meet new people, but Marsha says they're often cut off at the beginning once it's learned they are so religious. She doesn't feel that they preach, but Nick admits he seeks opportunities to talk about the Lord. He also took a drop in salary when he left a lucrative position at a private television network to become a director for a small Christian station. So their social gatherings consist of people very much like themselves—whether they want it that way or not. Nick says their situation is much like that of the reformed alcoholic whose drinking buddies don't come around anymore. Marsha says, with no trace of bitterness: "People don't want religion stuffed down their throats, but these are the very people who come to you in a crisis for help or prayers."

Their children are different too. They are expected to witness to Christ on the playground. Their daughter, because she's older, has explained her beliefs to her friends and they usually listen to her because, as Nick says, "kids are closer to God. They're not sophisticated." Their teachers understand that there are certain things the children can't take part in—such as dancing to disco records as part of health class. Nick and Marsha also object to any teaching of the theory of evolution, but they are not so adamant that they refuse their children a public school education. They are given a Christian perspective at home and taught that their parents care enough to say no to them. Nick prays with them each night and when there are problems, the family prays as a whole. The children read the Bible every day and are restricted in their television viewing and the music they listen to. "California is producing many of the programs and records," Nick says, "and it promulgates a life-style which says that whatever feels good, you do it. Because we're committed Christians we're not taken out of this world, but we're not totally part of this life system either." They all go to church every Sunday, at the moment a Pentecostal church, but they have no denominational preference. Nick says: "People are getting more and more shocked by the world and they realize something is wrong. I feel there is no other answer except Jesus Christ. And others can sniff and laugh if they want to."

It goes without saying that Nick and Marsha are monogamous. Nick has seen his colleagues turn to other women and end up with an emptiness, losing what he views as most precious: a home held together with love. He says so many people make the wrong moves, marrying for the wrong reasons. He wonders what has happened to the traditional value placed on a wife who will be a sensitive and good mother and a faithful companion. "I am flesh and blood," he says, "but you must maintain an attitude of love toward your kids and your wife. Every day you go into that jungle and you can be consumed or you can come back to live another day. The main objective of some people seems to be selfishness. They're only *looking* at love. There has to be a lot of patience and striving toward a quietness and sweetness in life. My marriage is not blissful every day but it is better than anything anyone else has to offer."

Nick admits he feels out of step, swimming against the tide, and that in itself can cause a peculiar kind of sorrow. No doubt he must appear to others to be an apostle of discipline but it has its compensations: "When you've looked toward God, you have an internal truth and you become clear-eyed." He and Marsha, he says, are not at all confused.

Conclusion
For a Long, Long Time

After all the interviews and the sorting out of so many thoughts, I think it is a reasonable statement that a large measure of self-discipline, tolerance, and forbearance gives marriage or any relationship the best possible chance for success. Forbearance seems a quaint word, but its meaning was made clear to me during an interview with a couple in a nursing home. They had been married sixty-four years and they were an obvious choice to impart some words of wisdom about love that lasts.

Although the husband was far more knowledgeable than his wife, he constantly kept his peace and played the quiet, passive audience to her nonstop chatter and grumbling. I could see that they were very much in love, and I asked them why they thought their marriage had been so enduring. Without hesitation, the husband said in a loud voice, "Forbearance!"

Endurance is closely linked with forbearance and I see it as a willingness to live with adversity. I think of a woman in her forties who came late to endurance; it was a quality she didn't know she possessed. When she learned of her husband's affair, her first reaction was to head for the front door. But she stopped just long enough to deal with some important insights. Although she was justifiably angry and hurt, she realized she had often taken her husband and her marriage for granted.

She had nagged often enough or been indifferent. Did this affair truly negate her husband's good qualities and the patience he had shown her in the past? "It was hard," she told me, "but I finally understood that we are responsible for a lot of things that happen to us. We can make excuses for the rest of our lives about why things didn't go right. But we let these things happen." This woman endured and she has a better marriage now.

Endurance is cloaked in many guises and some people would be hard pressed to understand why it may be the vital element in a relationship. Leslie knows all about it. She is a mature, independent woman who is an executive in a New York firm and has enjoyed brief sexual couplings during her travels; strictly out of physical necessity, she says, because her older husband is impotent. She understands thoroughly why she has decided to stay with him and it has nothing to do with pity. She is grateful for the vital supportive role he once played in her life and she would be less than human to walk out now. She does not believe in clinging to a destructive relationship but she admires people who continue to work at it when the thrill is gone. "It's surprising," she says, "how many men I've met who hang on to their marriages as tenaciously as women and for some of the same reasons. The kids, security, their shared past, but mostly because they're just as afraid of loneliness as the rest of us." Stated so bluntly, there may be no romance here, but for some people shared memories and kindness are fine enough. All of us have said at some time: "I don't know what keeps those two together." And very few of us will ever know.

I was impressed by the courage of some relationships. "Think," one woman in Vancouver demanded of me, "about the healthy partner who stands by while the other person physically or mentally deteriorates. I watched my mother wait hand and foot on my father for five years and I kept wishing she would leave him. He was so awful those last years, and when he died I still resented him. I see my mother now, a serene woman with her garden, who knows the contentment of having done the right thing. She taught me something without ever putting it into words. You don't abandon someone during a bad time when he has been most of your world." Another woman, who is caring for a sick husband many years her senior, said: "There are more noble ideas than you think and that's why some marriages stay together."

Still on the topic of endurance, a Winnipeg psychiatrist told me he is disgusted with the tendency to walk out on marriages that are basically sound. "They leave merely for the sake of change. They are unwilling to change within the relationship. It's easier to find someone to fit you than to fit yourself to someone else. There is no willingness to come together with their differences."

Now that it is presumably acceptable to live together, and have children out of wedlock, marriage as an institution is probably being examined more seriously than ever before. Very few people *have* to get married anymore for fear of social censure and a growing number consider it totally unnecessary. Not as many parents seem to have the nerve to ask their coupling offspring: "So when's the big day?" It's not that these parents don't believe in their own marriages, but they, too, are affected by changing social viewpoints, particularly the one that holds that equally fulfilling relationships without the awesome responsibilities exist outside the institution of marriage. I was told stories of compatible couples who married and suddenly became unsuitable as partners. This is what worries a Vancouver man who had been married unsuccessfully once and did not plan to now marry the girl he has been living with for six years. "It's the fearsome permanence, the lifelong commitment," he said. "There's the legality of marriage and the daily responsibility of making someone else happy."

For some people, it is undoubtedly a good thing that marriage is an option rather than the only means of expressing devotion and commitment. But marriage still is an enduring cornerstone and there is in our society a powerful urge for legitimacy, to make a formal and legal declaration that love *is* binding. A Los Angeles couple who married after living together two years said: "Marriage is one way of telling the world you are together and committed. There is no other ceremony. People don't take you seriously as a couple if you're just living together."

I found that the women's movement has affected all couples to some degree. More men are sharing in the housework and most feel guilty if they're not. Some are dismayed and sometimes threatened by the number of wives who are resuming careers or trying to acquire them. The stunning blow is the growing number of women who walk out of long-lasting relationships with no other explanation than that they need to find themselves. I had anguished conversations with three men in this situation. They all said they never saw it coming and their only explanation was that their wives were going out to become liberated.

Of course, it was more complicated than that. The real surprise is that more women know they have choices. Tim's experience was typical. His wife was quiet and acquiescent for twenty years of marriage and then one day, before he could understand what hit him, she was gone, living in a boardinghouse, working at a job meaningful to her, and drinking beer with taxi drivers at night. Even in his pain, he managed to be philosophical and said he still believes in marriage and monogamy but that marriage in the future will have to be more efficient in dealing with changing attitudes toward women and their roles. There is already more honesty between the sexes, he said. But there must be equality and less manipulation. There will always have to be compromise because, as Tim put it: "Short-term gains are rarely worth the long-term consequences." There is no question the women's movement has freed some women from intolerable situations, but it has also made housewives who don't want careers feel guilty. In some cases it has caused women whose marriages have been quite acceptable to them to abandon any notion of compromise—to risk everything for an elusive personal freedom and a variety of experiences *now*.

One of the hallmarks of people who have successful, long-lasting relationships is a sense of adventure in their sex lives and their goals. Two examples. A girlfriend of mine eagerly read *The Hite Report* and other literature on female orgasm and was astonished to discover she'd never had one. She became sexually aggressive and encouraged her husband to try new tactics. After all these years, they're into garter belts, dancing long into Saturday evenings, and God knows what else. Another couple, much older, gave up their solid careers, packed their possessions, and moved to Hawaii to start all over. As the husband said: "Where would I be at sixty-five? I'd be here in this house with fifteen years of the mortgage paid off. Helen and I are going into business together and that's going to be an interesting new relationship."

The area of greatest contention with all couples was sex. I found a high incidence of sexual infidelity with successful couples, but I also found an enormous tolerance for and often an acceptance of infidelity as inevitable. Some people insisted that loyalty is more important than fidelity, and I was interested in how they were able to separate the two. Others argued convincingly that trust and commitment cannot exist without fidelity. Except for one couple that is experimenting with an open marriage, everyone agreed that affairs cause pain and do a certain amount of damage to the relationship. Nevertheless, some partners were able to assess what went wrong and to look at the positive aspects of their relationships.

Every marriage expert I spoke to said that a few acts of infidelity should never lead to divorce if there's something worth salvaging, and it was not difficult at all to find people who came back stronger and wiser after affairs. The experts agree that there are many happy monogamous couples today and monogamy is valued by far more people than polls might indicate. But there is also a feeling that faithfulness is not necessarily tenable or even healthy in our society. Fidelity is a personal choice that some, but certainly not all, couples make.

The matter of jealousy is totally bound up with the question of sexual fidelity. Some regarded it as a bleak emotion which could be overcome; that seems to be the "modern" approach. Others, less "liberated," said jealousy was stamped into the human psyche and all one could do was try to curb it. In my interviews, I didn't find any couples who had managed to eradicate jealousy, but I did find some who had come to see it as a healthy emotion, one that works as a signal to get ready for something. A Philadelphia psychiatrist told me, "Jealousy means you are in danger of losing something and you're scared. How can you eliminate an emotion like that?" My conclusion is that it can't and perhaps needn't be overcome; the best attitude is to learn to live with it.

Yes, learning to live with it. In the end, I found myself returning to a very simple point. Being in love is easy and happens all the time. Loving is a learning and striving process that takes a lifetime.